PHILOSOPHICAL EVENTS

John Rajchman

PHILOSOPHICAL EVENTS

ESSAYS OF THE '80s

Columbia University Press
NEW YORK

Columbia University Press
New York   Oxford
Copyright © 1991 Columbia University Press
All rights reserved

Library of Congress Cataloging-in-Publication Data

Rajchman, John.
Philosophical events : essays of the '80s / John Rajchman.
p.   cm.
Includes bibliographical references and index.
ISBN 0-231-07210-4
1. Philosophy, Modern—20th century.   I. Title.
B804.R26   1990   190'.9'048—dc20   90-41307
CIP

Casebound editions of Columbia University Press books are Smyth-sewn
and printed on permanent and durable acid-free paper

∞

Printed in the United States of America

c 10 9 8 7 6 5 4 3 2 1

CONTENTS

PREFACE

The '80s was a decade of rethinking, revision, regrouping. Following a crisis in global utopian ideals, there arose a debate about the very nature and tradition of critical thought, and its relation to the Enlightenment and to Democracy. Three new kinds of philosophy confronted one another: "neopragmatist," "poststructuralist," and "communications-theoretical," and their confrontation served to redraw the old geographical map that had made of the Atlantic or the Channel a philosophical divide. At the same time there arose a debate over new forms of art and culture in a period of electronic technologies and a triumphant consumerism. A new label was invented, "postmodernism," coined in America, but soon to have currency almost everywhere.

In all these controversies we may perhaps discern an attempt, frought with uncertainty and many antagonisms, to find again in the historical events of the Enlightenment, or Democracy, or Modernism in European culture, a new starting point for something as yet unfinished in our traditions. For we examined those events in new ways and from new angles, and sought in them not "the end of history," but a new start within it. We were concerned not with the ending of a great story, but with events in a complex history;

events which we may not yet know how to name, but which come "after" Stalinism, Fascism, and the War, in a "postmodern" world. It is the chance or possibility of such events in the history in which we find ourselves, which supplies the central question of these essays.

This book owes much to Foucault. I develop what in an earlier book I called his "historical nominalism" in terms of a reflection on what an *event* is. In his work Foucault held to a "principle of singularity," which simply says that "there are events in thought." It was this principle that guided his questioning of our inherited ways of being. Foucault wanted to open the space of a critical questioning that would be prior to who, at a time and place, we think we are, universally, necessarily, transcendentally, or teleologically. What seems "universal" about our experience would not be what accounts for what we think or do, but what needs to be critically accounted for in it. Thus Foucault proposed to regard the "discourses" through which we think and act as *events* of a particular kind. To expose such categories of our experience as our "sexuality" or our "deviancy" as singular events in our thought, was to help open the critical but undetermined possibility of other conceptions—to start up again the history of our own self-conceptions, to "eventalize" that history and ask again, "who are we today?"

Even Foucault's last and literally unfinished work had this critical aim: to understand our ethical "practices of the self" as events, and to ask what new ways of speaking critically of ourselves, what new sorts of "spirituality" are open to us today. ". . . to rethink the Greeks today consists not in valorizing Greek morality as the domain of morality *par excellence* which one would need for self-reflection, but in seeing to it that European thought can get started again on Greek thought as an experience given once, and in regard to which one can be totally free."[1]

The conception of "event" that runs throughout this series of overlapping essays from the '80s is of this "nominalist" sort. An event is not, something as Aristotle thought, a narrative sequence of words and deeds occurring within a setting and organized by a plot. It is rather a moment of erosion, collapse, questioning, or problematization of the very assumptions of the setting within which a drama may take place, occasioning the chance or possibility of another, different setting. It is thus like those turning points in a tragedy that suspend the drama and the world its protagonists inhabit, as when Shakespeare says, "time is out of joint"; it is like those events in a drama which take the drama itself as an event. It is not defined by a fixed beginning and end, but is something that occurs in the midst of a history, causing us to redistribute our sense of what has gone before it and what might come after. An event is thus not something one inserts into an emplotted dramatic sequence with its start and finish, for it initiates a new sequence that retrospectively determines its beginnings, and which leaves its ends unknown or undetermined.

We ourselves are not prior to events of this kind. They are on the contrary just those occurrences which cause us to ask again what we might still become. But while events thus question our identifications, our "solidarities," the agreements on which our practices rest, they do not confront us as a crushing fate or necessity. On the contrary, they expose that something we previously took to be necessary in fact no longer is. They appeal to our freedom. The experience of freedom is an experience of events, an experience not of what we must be or do, but of new possibilities of being and doing. The task of a critical intellectual is then to "see," to expose, to analyze these events that happen to us in the midst of our histories, freeing the space for other histories. It is a task that requires a critical use of history to save us from the historicism that asks us to return to the past and the progressivism that tells us what must come in the future. But the question of events is also the question of the invention of ourselves. It requires the creation of new spaces, of new "forums," for reflection and analysis, in which to open again the possibilities of what we may think, do, or be.

The events of 1968 and those that are happening in Eastern Europe as I am writing have been called "revolutions." And yet they are not so like what happened in 1789 or 1917. Rather they cause us to ask again what those "revolutions" were. They cause us to see them not so much as stories with a beginning and an end, but as events from which to start again something as yet unsettled. Perhaps we might see 1968 (with its new questions about women and the relations between the sexes, about minorities and racism, about deviancy and normality, the environment and technology), and 1989 (with its new questions about the ideals of socialism and the historical constitution of the warfare-welfare nation state) as dates not of the process of Revolution, but, in their relations with one another, as dates of those unforeseen events that change our historical sense, and so call for the exercise of our critical intelligence.

NOTES

1. "The Return of Morality," in *Foucault Live* (Semiotext(e), 1989), p. 325.

PHILOSOPHICAL EVENTS

Part I

PHILOSOPHICAL TRADITIONS

ONE

Translation Without a Master

TRADITIONS AND TRANSLATIONS

In recent years, there has been lots of dispute in philosophy about philosophy itself—its aims, its history, its social and political responsibilities, and the sort of relation it has to other kinds of discourse, aesthetic, scientific, or political. With this discussion has gone the sense of the end, or dead end, of one kind of philosophy or another, even sometimes of philosophy itself as we have known it.

These disputes have not been restricted to one country or one kind of philosophy. In particular they have accompanied changes in three different traditions: (1) the changes in English-language philosophy Cornel West and I provisionally termed "post-analytic philosophy"; (2) the changes in German language philosophy associated with a second generation of critical theorists, notably Habermas, and (3) the changes in French-language philosophy that have collectively come to be known as "poststructuralism." In each of these cases the question of philosophy itself has been raised, and an attempt been made to revise or renew its history.

This lecture was given at a symposium, "Philosophy and Translation," organized by David Wood, University of Warwick, July 1988. Proceedings forthcoming from Routledge Press.

More recently still, we have witnessed among the three a series of exchanges, clashes, critical readings and misreadings, confrontations and adaptations that have cut across the Rhine, the Channel, and the Atlantic. They raise the question of whether there has been, if not a break-up then a loosening or reshuffling of the boundaries geographical, historical, or linguistic, that not so long ago seemed to divide up contemporary philosophy. I am not saying that people are not, or should not be, continuing to work in the traditions or with the problems thought to be delimited by these boundaries. On the contrary, the more original work that is done in these traditions, the richer the possibilities of exchange or of interference among them. Nevertheless I think there has been a sort of "de-nationalization" of philosophical work. There is now analytic philosophy done in German and French, and critical theory or deconstruction done in English. Habermas' work is now in many respects closer to Rawls or Peirce than it is to Derrida, who, for his part, has helped to initiate new readings in French of Adorno and Benjamin—authors who formed Habermas' thought. Similarly there is a whole aspect of Foucault's work that is closer to Kuhn than it is to Husserl, Hegel, or even Nietzsche, and another aspect closer to Weber than it is to Sartre or Derrida. With these realignments has gone the sense that the story of contemporary philosophy itself might be retold—the way it took shape in the '30s, the divisions that were established after the War, the way new directions emerged in the '60s, and the way in the '80s these changes came to confront one another. In any case, the three authors I will consider, Habermas, Rorty, and Foucault, have each reflected on this complex contemporary history, and defined his work in terms of it.

To put a date on it, the phase of confrontation and exchange may be said to have started about ten years ago, in '78 or '79. Nineteen seventy-nine was the date of *The Postmodern Condition* of Lyotard. It was the date of *Philosophy and the Mirror of Nature* of Rorty. And it was at this time as well that Habermas began his essays about modernity, and Foucault his reflections on the question of enlightenment. Nineteen seventy-eight was also the date of a work less well known than these: *The Literary Absolute* of Nancy and Lacoue-Labarthe. This book was, or contained, a translation in the ordinary sense—a translation of the fragmentary writings of the Jena Romantics, and it initiated a series of translations into French of works from the post-Kantian literary and philosophical traditions of Germany. But the book might also be said to be a sort of "philosophical translation" in the genealogical style which asks what the event of Romanticism means for who we are today. In this respect it is linked to Rorty, who, of course, presents us with pragmatism as the "successor-movement" to Romanticism.

Worries about the nature of philosophy, pronouncements that one strain or another is at an end, rivalrous exchanges among contemporary kinds—all this is not new. It is quite normal in philosophy. New objects of discussion, new styles of argument or analysis are invented, and the question arises of how they are related to other ones, in the past or in the present. A new philosophy attacks fresh problems, applying to them fresh concepts, which discover new sorts of application. In what does this novelty consist, and how does one pass from the old to the new? by a radical refusal and a new beginning? by a subsumption in a higher synthesis or superior method of analysis? or by a rediscovery of something forgotten that promises a recommencement? Such are the questions of the unity and the history of philosophies, and they are raised anew today.

For Habermas, Rorty, and Foucault may each be said to advance a new way of doing philosophy, even if it is one others say is not new or not philosophy. Each tells a story in which there is a break in the tradition, or the ending of something in it, and each uses his story to say something about the others. Thus there is common ground, even if the novelties, the stories, and the exchanges are quite different or even at odds with one another. We may thus ask whether there is an event of which the three, in their differences, participate—a sort of "crisis" of which each may be read as offering a different "diagnosis"; and further, we may wonder whether this crisis is a creative one, whether it itself will produce anything new.

Since the heyday of the philological study of antiquity, translation between languages had regularly been used to conceptualize the changes in the history of philosophies. An analogy is set up between translation and the sorts of interpretative relations a new philosophy would have with others, past or present. If, for example, we suppose a radical disunity of philosophies, and radical dissociations in its history, then it is said that there can be no "translations" in philosophy at all. For then there would be no common ground, no "common sense." To translate is by definition to suppose some common ground between the two languages of the translation. If it is sense that translation preserves, where there is translation, there can be no *altogether* new sense. There is always some sense in common.

But novelty may be regarded in terms of an "anomaly of sense." There is anomaly when one comes across something that "problematizes" the assumptions with which one normally proceeds. In particular, an anomaly can cause us to question those presumptions which we would otherwise never give up in translating. Interpretive relations among different philosophies old and new might thus be modeled on this situation where there arises in a translation something undecipherable by the conventions used to translate, which opens those conventions themselves to revision. Two philosophies may then be said to be "incommensurable" when their confrontation with each other leads to such an anomaly. And such incommensurability may be said to be "creative" when it gives rise to something new.

There is thus another sense of "common sense," or of what is common in a "philosophical translation." It is put in an empiricist fashion by Paul Feyerabend when he says that the public would be best off if it let there be a proliferation of incommensurable traditions. Proliferation is not a matter of a classifiable plurality that is tolerated. The disunity of traditions is dynamic. We will never yet know what new traditions may come. The question then arises of whether there is not a way of letting two or more traditions interfere with one another, bringing them together at just those incommensurable points where they diverge. Does there exist a mode of thinking in which two traditions are so linked as to expose in a new way what differentiates them, or in which, as it were, it is their difference that they have in common? To this question belongs another. Can there exist a common sense, a public, or public space —a *glasnost*—which is not identified with a single tradition, or with a single way of classifying the plurality of traditions, but which is so divided up that each tradition remains exposed to the singularities of the others, and of those yet to come? Can there exist a philosophical community not based in the assumptions of an overarching unity?

If one then *starts* with an anomaly or a problematization in one's thinking, marking an "incommensurability" with others past or present, one finds oneself in a situation where the language *into* which one will end up translating will never be identical to the one with which one starts. Such would be the creative situation of what might be called "translation without a master." And this lack of mastery, this freedom might be contrasted with, and used to analyze, two other situations or images of translation: that of *fidelity*, where the other is the master and the problem is one of identification with his word; and that of *charity*, where one can't help being oneself the master, and the problem is the altruistic one of knowing what should be, or should have been, good or true for the other. For it is the freedom of translation that allows us to discern the obsessional side of fidelity (no other set of words can ever be adequate to that of the master) and the autistic side of charity (nothing in the words of the other can alter the basic representations one uses to identify oneself). Conversely, translation without a master would be the art of breaking with those with whom one nevertheless identifies, while exposing oneself to the singularities of those one nevertheless tries to understand. Put more pointedly, my question is then whether our current situation of clash and exchange is, or may be regarded as, such a creative or open situation of the lack of a philosophical master, and whether it might therefore be productive of something new.

HABERMAS' MODERNITY

Habermas' lectures on the philosophies of modernity advance a new history of what has happened since Kant. The motivation for it, he says, came from the challenge of the "neostructuralists." By that he means the writings of such people as Foucault and Derrida, primarily from the '60s and early '70s. He proposes to meet the challenge by inserting this work within a discourse comprising the various attempts to justify "modern" society and articulate its fundamental divisions, without any reference to "tradition." His central claim is that such "discourse of modernity" has been constitutive of philosophy since at least Hegel, who derived it from the version of the conflict between the ancients and the moderns propounded in the German aesthetics of the eighteenth century. That the French authors in question never viewed their work in terms of this "discourse" is the mark of the novelty, or incommensurability, that comes from Habermas' confrontation with them.

In inserting the French into this new story of post-Kantian thought, Habermas is not much interested in what they say about themselves, or the contexts from which their work arose. Indeed the very category of "neostructuralism" is a curious if familiar one.

7

Nobody has ever called *himself* a neostructuralist, especially not in France where neostructuralism would have been born. And when Habermas goes on to say that the French neostructuralists resemble the young or neo-conservatives of Germany, he is inadvertently as informative about the German context in which the French authors have been read as about the authors themselves.

For there is a general principle of Habermas' revised history. Nothing *new* has been added by the French philosophers to the German philosophers who preceded them. Just where Foucault or Derrida thought they were making a new departure from post-Kantian thought, Habermas says they were only repeating it. Thus he declares "Derrida wants to go beyond Heidegger, fortunately he goes back behind him";[1] and of Foucault's "ingenious" discussion of the "anthropological slumbers" of modern philosophy, Habermas says that it was "already analyzed by Schiller, Fichte, Schelling and Hegel in a similar fashion."[2] It follows that the French thinkers are only weak or belated "translations" of an earlier German philosophy. What is new is rather the ending of the tradition to which the French have contributed nothing.

In Habermas' new story there is a basic question: how today to "reassure" ourselves philosophically or to define who or what we are in philosophical terms. The question arises at a particular time —that of "modernity," or when ancient or speculative sorts of self-definition are no longer available to us. And then there is a bad way of responding to the question: in terms of "subject-centered reason," or when people define themselves with a philosophy of consciousness, or with a theory of any sort of subject that would alienate or produce or realize itself in history.

It is Habermas' view that until his own "universal pragmatics," virtually all the philosophers of modernity set out on this bad "road" even though, at what Habermas calls the "crossroads" in their thinking, we now see they need not have. It is here that we find Habermas' version of the theme of the end of philosophy. He says the various versions of subject-centered reason have all gone nowhere, ending in bankruptcy or insoluable difficulties. The moral of the story is that subject-centered reason is no reason at all.

Habermas' story is thus self-centered. It issues in and so justifies his own views. At the same time it presupposes them. This is what might be called "Habermas' circle" and it helps explain the sometimes bombastic exhilaration of having found the solution to a problem that bedeviled all the rest of modern philosophy. This

"self-assurance" matches with the central problem it defines: the
lack of philosophical self-confidence characteristic of modernity.
The core of what Habermas says we moderns have always needed
to reassure ourselves is an intersubjective transcendental philosophy, and the institutions of social democracy, the first supplying
the philosophical grounding for the norms of the second—just
what Habermas himself is now prepared to offer us.

Armed with this self-assuring insight into the self-defeating
character of much of modern philosophy, Habermas concludes that
we must now set some limits on any critical questioning of ourselves and our tradition. We must never again question ourselves
without instancing and defending an intersubjective norm of judgment. For to do otherwise is to fall prey to just the sort of "aestheticism" through which the tradition was led astray. And that is
precisely the danger and the predicament of Foucault, Derrida, and
the other unnamed neostructuralists. Foucault is a "cryptonorma-
tivist," Derrida an "aesthetic decisionist," and as such these philosophers court two dangers the tradition has exposed. There is the
danger of anti-liberalism (they can't question the tradition as they
do and support democratic struggles), and a danger of irrationalism (they can't question the tradition as they do, and retain their
reason, or continue to "communicate"). Thus to the degree that
Foucault and Derrida are prepared to support the achievements of
enlightened democracy, Habermas says they must be contradicting
themselves. With this danger of an anti-democratic irrationalism
one senses that one is close to an event and a fear that fuels Habermas' revised account of the tradition—the event and the fear of
fascism.[3]

In short, the sort of exchange with the neostructuralists Habermas works out in his lectures on modernity might be said to be
informed by an agenda that could be put in some such terms as
these. The evil of German fascism has shown us the dangers of
"subject-centered reason." Since Kant, a central source of this dangerous kind of reason has been the great philosophical histories of
modernity, and it is now urgent that we purge this tendency from
the inheritance of German philosophy. So far one has a view that
would be familiar to many American analytic philosophers who
are also liberals. But Habermas adds: in Paris the lesson of modernity has not been learned; there the dangerous influence of Heidegger, Nietzsche, and Freud continues to flourish. Thus the French
have become the bad Romantic Germans, and it now falls to the

Germans, or at least the West Germans, to show the French the path to become good Americans—which is to say at once rationalist and liberal, or social democratic.

RORTY'S IRONY

But all liberals are not rationalists, at least not in the transcendental sense Habermas gives to the term. Richard Rorty is the first, but not the second. He is my second case.

In 1979, in *Philosophy and the Mirror of Nature*, Rorty told a story about the internal collapse of a central paradigm in postwar American philosophy of language, knowledge, and mind, and he set this story within a larger and European crisis in the history of Western thought since Plato. There was thus the ending of something—foundational thought—and the beginning of something new—conversation. At the time Rorty was an analytically trained philosopher at Princeton who was intent on opening this philosophy up, and connecting it to recent Continental work, particularly that of the "poststructuralists," who, at this time, were largely ignored in the analytic profession.

Rorty devised an original way of discussing Foucault and Derrida, one in which they were seen to share common ground with what he then saw as the collapse of analytic philosophy. In both cases, he said, there was opposition to "foundations" or the view that there exist representations privileged by the fact that they mirror some independent essential reality. Accordingly, he enlisted the support of the French authors in his quarrels with "Kantian epistemologically-centered philosophy." He dreamt of a "postphilosophical culture" heralded in Europe by Nietzsche and Heidegger, but in America by Emerson and Dewey. When analytic philosophers found out that this was what was being said by the likes of Foucault or Derrida, there were not a few who were happy to have grounds to dismiss them. For it must be said that while Rorty likes to think of himself as a philosopher of solidarity, his story of the demise of analytic philosophy in American context can hardly be said to have commanded wide assent.

The story of American philosophy which Rorty tried to insert into the larger tradition was itself a story of exchange with European philosophy, in which one might discern three stages. First, starting in the '30s, there is a process of the absorption of the work of the emigré German and Viennese philosophers who would eventually overtake the American profession, resulting in something presenting itself as "Anglo-American." Second, Rorty argued that the way this work had been taken up and "translated" in America contained the seeds of its demise—such would be the achievement, if not the intent, of Quine, Davidson, and Kuhn. And finally, in this internal collapse, there would lie the possibility of a rediscovery and renewal of the pragmatist tradition which these European philosophers had momentarily eclipsed—a pragmatism more of Dewey than Peirce, according to which truth is a wholly extrinsic matter of changing practices of agreement with no deeper intrinsic or philosophical foundation. The hope for this last phase is one which, as Cornel West points out, occurs very early on in Rorty's writings—in the '60s. But in 1979 Rorty was prepared to ally this post-analytic Deweyan pragmatism with those portions of European or Continental philosophy, which, in questioning the tradition, might be thought to have supplanted a philosophy of foundation with a philosophy of conversation. This is the maneuver that strikes Habermas (who finds something of his own theory of universal pragmatics not in Dewey but in Peirce) as a "beclouding" of "the sober insights of pragmatism" with the "Nietzschean pathos of a *Lebensphilosophie* that has made the linguistic turn."[4]

The sort of "conversation" upon which Rorty embarked after these dramatic and widely discussed claims, may be said in no small part to be a work of contemporary international exchange and "translation." It was as though a central residual function for thought in a "post-philosophical culture" was this "translational" one. Announcing the demise of all foundational thought, Rorty quit Princeton and set out on a period of travels, engaging in a style of philosophical journalism, in which he came to apply to the international scene a strategy he had used with success within analytic philosophy: that of mapping the terrain of a debate, splitting the difference between various positions. Thus he wrote up little "conversations"—imaginary dialogues with or among contemporary European philosophers in which they and "we" were invited to resolve our differences by adopting Rorty's own neo-pragmatist views.

In these dialogical mappings, Rorty's own voice became more distinctive, and acquired a more secure place. And just as his "first person" became more distinctive and more singular, Rorty became increasingly preoccupied with the theme of "solidarity." In his "conversations" there emerges a constant, if somewhat fluctuating *solicitation* of solidarity, or agreement with himself. He wrote to invite solidarity just where there was none apparent. The hope that there could be such agreement, combined with the sense that there would not, conspired to give Rorty's work its distinctive tone of blunt and sanctimonious sarcasm.

In the sketches contained in these post-philosophical conversations, certain features stand out. Rorty took Habermas' point that neostructuralist thought was in some way incompatible with democratic values. He gave up a projected work on Heidegger. He downplayed the theme of the end of philosophy—even of analytic philosophy—identifying it instead with Foucault and Derrida. Focusing on John Dewey, he came to see in the renewal of pragmatism a way of espousing democracy while dispensing with the assurances of a foundational or transcendental philosophy. To this hybrid view, he came to attach the old label of "liberalism."

In this manner, Rorty's "conversations" offered him a way to split the difference between Habermas and the neostructuralists. At the same time, it allowed him to sort out his own motivations, mixing polite English liberal values with the radical questioning of the philosophical tradition he had found in Heidegger or in the French authors. He drew up a distinction between private or literary, and public or political, interests or spheres. Thus he presented the French figures as private, literary ironical thinkers who ought never to have confused their work with politics, and in particular, with any questioning of "liberalism." On the other side he presented Habermas as someone who agrees with the only position "we" should have in politics—"liberalism"—but who found it necessary to back it up with an unnecessary transcendental theory of communication, which threatened to deprive "us" of pursuing literary irony in the privacy of our homes, studies, or seminars.

Thus the larger sort of "mapping" Rorty came to in his post-philosophical travels might be put in this way: if only the French would stick to being private ironical Romantics, and the Germans would realize they don't need Kant or transcendental philosophy to be liberals, "we" could all live happily together as good American pragmatists.

FOUCAULT'S QUESTION

Foucault's *The Order of Things* of 1966 was also about an ending of something in philosophy and social science, namely, "Man," or foundational anthropology. And this ending was the start of something new—the possibility of a critical examination of the history of discourses without anthropological guarantees or assumptions. Philosophy, he said at the time, should become a "diagnostic activity." It should diagnose new possibilities in thought which arise when there is a questioning of something basic formerly taken for granted as given—such as the definition of ourselves as "Man."

Retrospectively it is interesting to note that the view of contemporary philosophy he thus presents in the last chapters of *The Order of Things* first occurs in his unpublished introduction to his translation of the *Anthropology from a Pragmatic Point of View* of Kant, which comprised his thesis under Jean Hippolyte in 1961.[5] It is, of course, to Kant that we owe the first uses of the term "pragmatism" in philosophy, and Foucault stresses that the "pragmatic point of view" in anthropology differed from what Kant had called the "practical" one—the suprasensible realm or republic of moral or legal agents. The pragmatic point of view discovered aspects of life and language that could not be captured by a formal theory of right or property. It discovered another kind of "world" from the practical one—a world not of *Seele* or of *Geist* but of *Gemüt*, a world of macrobiotics and madness, in which what counts is not one's transcendental identity but rather how, concretely, in the pragmatic world, one proceeds to make oneself and become who one is.

It could be said that in his "diagnoses of the present" Foucault never stopped being preoccupied with how this sort of pragmatic world had been, and could yet again be, integrated into the practice of a critical thought. That is why he said in his 1961 introduction that this particular work into which Kant had interpolated material from all phases of his thought, from the pre-critical to the posthumous, was at once marginal and essential to critical philosophy itself.

This problem is raised again in any case in the writings from around '78 or '79, when Foucault returns to another apparently marginal work in the Kantian corpus: Kant's paper on the question "What is Enlightenment." That paper would be the start of a long and entangled tradition in critical thought, of which Foucault's own "diagnoses of the present" would be one outcome. In his account of this tradition, we find Foucault's first references to the Frankfurt School as a kind of critical thought. It thus offers a sense of Foucault's attitude toward the exchange or clash of contemporary philosophies that was taking shape during those years.

Foucault says that Kant's paper introduced a new *question* into

13

philosophy around which formed a new and historical "pole" of philosophical activity.

> This question is very different from the traditional philosophical questions: what is man? what is truth? how can we know something? and so on. The question which arises at the end of the eighteenth century is: what are we in our actuality? You will find this question in a text by Kant ... a new pole had been constitued for the activity of philosophizing, and this pole is characterized by the question, the permanent and everchanging question, "what are we today?" And that is, I think the field of the historical reflection on ourselves. Kant, Fichte, Hegel, Nietzsche, Max Weber, Husserl, Heidegger, the *Frankfurtschule* had tried to answer this question.[6]

Foucault observes that this kind of philosophical reflection about ourselves and the kinds of reason of which we are capable had been raised in different ways in different European countries. "The Enlightenment" was a different thing in each country. He mentions three: "Undoubtedly we should ask why this question of the Enlightenment without ever disappearing had such a different destiny in Germany, France, and the Anglo-Saxon countries, why here and there it was invested in such different domains and according to such varied chronologies."[7]

Weber had distinguished types of rationality in a history that took the Reformation as a privileged moment, and "the spirit of capitalism" as a central problem. But the French historians of science Bachelard and Canguilhem had distinguished yet other divisions in reason with other chronologies. Foucault stresses this plurality in the kinds of reason. To ask about enlightenment is to divide our rationality up. The question of enlightenment should not be seen as a question about reason itself, or about the constitutive features of the whole society in which it figures. For we can no longer think of philosophy as the determinant figure of a whole epoch, and an epoch as the realization of that philosophy.

One reason Foucault introduces Bachelard and Canguilhem into the picture is the importance their work was to acquire in France in the 1960s "when a 'crisis' began concerning not only the university, but also the status and the role of knowledge."[8] This crisis would explain how the careful, detailed, and somewhat austere writings of Canguilhem should have suddenly seemed central to Marxism, to psychoanalysis, and to sociology. But during these same years and in relation to this same "crisis" we find something of a parallel development in both Germany and America.

In America, Kuhn was at one with the French historians: he thought we must qualify our sense of modern science as a single monolithic event in our culture, and therefore in our "historical reflection on ourselves." His book was about scientific revolutions in the plural. There could be as many revolutions as there were "paradigms" of scientific research. The concept of the paradigm of a community with its journals, its textbooks, its institutes, and its internal debates was designed to incorporate both the "externalist" history typified by the Weberian historian Thomas Merton, and the "internalist" history typified by the French historian of ideas Alexandre Koyré. The "French" and the "German" traditions were thus brought together in 1962 in America in a new picture of a scientific community.

The publication of the *Structure of Scientific Revolutions* (a year after Foucault's history of madness and his translation of Kant had quietly appeared in France) helped introduce a new and historical "image of science" that was to shift the grounds in America from the philosophy the emigré Germans had brought with them, introducing into it new questions about the incommensurability, the realism, and the unity of scientific research. In France, in the '60s, Althusser had seen in Bachelard and Canguilhem a new way of returning to Marx. In America, in the same years, Rorty saw in Kuhn a new way of returning to Dewey. In the Vietnam decade, rationality seemed in question for the first time in American analytic philosophy.

But Foucault says that the French history of science goes back to the '30s when contemporary philosophy took shape in France. Starting in those years, Foucault traces a line separating a philosophy of rationality from a philosophy of consciousness, the tradition of Jean Cavaillès from the tradition of Sartre, or again two directions assumed by the reading of the *Cartesian Meditations* which Husserl delivered in Paris in 1929. In this division we find something not so unlike what would later become institutionalized and nationalized in America as the division between analytic and Continental philosophy. For, starting in the '30s, Cavaillès had taken up the work of Frege, Wittgenstein, and Carnap. He had espoused their critique of psychologism, and set out to study the foundations of mathematics.

We might then extend the lineages in Foucault's history into the

confrontations of our contemporary situation in the following sche-
matic fashion. In the '30s, before "positivism" got its bad name,
there arose a critique of psychologism and of historicism, and a
debate ensued over the logic of science or of scientific reasoning.
The "question of enlightenment" was posed not in terms of history
or of consciousness, but in terms of deductive or inductive patterns
of inference, and a theory of meaning. This kind of critical reflection on our rationality then came under fire in the '60s in France,
Germany, and America in three different ways, which led to new
historical ways of analyzing scientific reasoning. In France, there
was the renewal of the work of Canguilhem and Bachelard, to
which Althusser gave new impetus, and of which Foucault was one
outcome. In Germany, there was a renewal of the critique of "administrative reason," and the "positivism dispute" with Popper, of
which Habermas is one outcome. And in Anglo-Saxon countries
there was Kuhn's new image of science that initiated a debate, of
which Rorty is one outcome.

These three developments of the question of enlightenment in
the crisis years of the '60s may then be said to be the ones that
were to confront one another in the '80s. A rich and complex history would thus stand behind the confrontation. Habermas would
say the critique of administrative reason had been one-sided, and
that a proper account of the "interests" of Reason, and their division in modernity, would provide a new space for universal communication. Rorty would see in the paradigms of Kuhn's professional communities a new pragmatism in which all transcendental
reflection would end. And Foucault, for his part, would attempt to
continue the critical history of reason in a new key, concerned not
with universal conditions of possibility of a transcendental subject,
but rather with specific and changing "positivities" of reason. Thus
he states his own archeological and genealogical formulation of the
question of enlightenment, or of who we are today, in these terms:

> It will not seek to identify the universal structures of all knowl-
> edge or of all possible moral action, but will seek to treat the
> instances of discourse that articulate what we think, say, and do
> as so many historical events . . . it will not deduce from the form
> of what we are what it is impossible for us to do and to know,
> but it will separate out, from the contingency that has made us
> what we are, the possibility of no longer being, doing or thinking
> what we are, do or think.[9]

Foucault avoided confrontation. He said his kind of critical reflection on our history need not *preclude* the others, and that they
should not preclude his, as in what he called "the blackmail of the
Enlightenment." Yet his very way of envisaging the tradition comes
from his own thought: he sees an endless plurality in the question
of reason in our historical reflection on ourselves.

Foucault distinguishes the *question* of enlightenment from the
antiquarian study of the period of the Enlightenment. For it is
always a question about who we are *today*. Thus "the question" is
such as to always survive those formulations of it precise enough
to yield solid historical results, and conversely, the tradition maintains itself only by constantly reformulating the question that con-
stitutes it. The "today" in the question thus marks a particular
moment; it is always *actuel* in the sense that it remains open for we
who would take it up anew. Foucault's own attempt to devise a
kind of critical historical questioning prior to judgment by reference to agreed norms is tied up with this peculiar "historicity,"
in which a question would take precedence over the responses
given to it.

The question is prior. It is also anonymous. It "poses itself" and
its tradition confronts one in the anonymous form of "one has been
asking" or "it has been asked." It follows that *we* are not prior to
the question. Thus Foucault remarks:

> R. Rorty points out that in these analyses I do not appeal to any
> "we"—to any of those "we"s' whose consensus, whose values,
> whose traditions constitute the framework for a thought and
> define the conditions in which it can be validated. But the prob-
> lem is, precisely, to decide if it is actually suitable to place
> oneself within a "we" in order to assert the principles one recog-
> nizes and the values one accepts, or, if it is not rather necessary
> to make the future formation of a "we" possible by elaborating
> the question. Because it seems to me that the "we" must not be
> previous to the question, it can only be the result—and the
> necessarily temporary result—of the question as it is posed in
> the new terms in which one formulates it.[10]

It is just this anonymity which Rorty, as a philosopher of ethnic
solidarities, finds objectionable, seeing in it alternatively Foucault's "detached" tone, or pseudo-objectivity, or Foucault's mysticism, or longing for the transcendence of a new "event" in our
thought or our action. But Foucault's "anonymity" consists in this:

17

the question of enlightenment is not the property of any one group, it being open to formulation by different ones, and, in particular to ones that cut across national boundaries. This is the case for the example Foucault offers Rorty:

> I'm not sure that at the time when I wrote the history of madness there was a preexisting and receptive "we" to which I would only have had to refer in order to write my book, and of which this book would have been the spontaneous expression. Laing, Cooper, Basaglia and I had no community, nor any relationship. But the problem posed itself to those who had read us, as it also posed itself to some of us, of seeing if it was possible to establish a "we" on the basis of work that had been done, a "we" that would also be likely to form a community of action.[11]

This sort of situation in which a question "poses itself" in several different places, even different countries, in such a way as to form a new community of action, is, more generally, one Foucault associates with the struggles of the '60s.

> They are "transversal" struggles, that is, they are not limited to one country. Of course they develop more easily and to a greater extent in certain countries, but they are not confined to a particular political or economical form of government.[12]

This anonymity and priority of "the question," whose successive formulations would lead up to our contemporary situation, thus suggests one sort of contrast. While Rorty holds out the hope that solidarity with what is best in the West should turn out to be nothing else than solidarity with Thomas Jefferson or John Dewey, and that America might thus find itself at the center of a revision of philosophical geography, and while Habermas thinks the only way out of Romantic nationalism is through an ascendence to the norms of a universal pragmatics of speech, in Foucault, we observe the workings of another view. The "we" of Foucault's question is not the consensual "we" of practical reason, nor the ironical one of liberal solidarity. It is the "we" of the anonymity of the question, whose image of critical thought is preceded neither by an international or transnational foundation of norms, nor by a national identification with a single tradition. It is rather a community of those who would constantly expose their own thought to an experience of *de-nationalization*. And it is perhaps precisely the possibility of this anonymity and this de-nationalization that lies at the heart of the fears and the anxieties we so often encounter when the purity of a nation or of its traditions is asserted or assumed.

In short, in the case of Foucault we might say: if only Habermas would allow in history, and in particular in the present, moments of critical questioning prior to the norms rational agents may agree upon, and Rorty, such a critical questioning prior to pragmatic solidarities, we might be able to let each of these different practices of enlightenment proliferate, temporarily hooking up with one another, and so dissolving the nationalist boundaries of the traditions of their provenance.

TRANSLATION WITHOUT A MASTER

One thing that is new in these three cases of contemporary philosophy is then just the sense of the opening of the tradition, or the requirement of a revision and a renewal. As a style of philosophy, critical thought is again up for grabs. The common ground is this sense of erosion of common grounds.

For Habermas, what is new is the realization that there can be no other reasoned or philosphical attitude to our "modernity" than that of his universal pragmatics. For the only alternative, subject-centered reason, has shown itself to be both dangerous and bankrupt or self-defeating. In taking up the challenge of the "neostructuralists" Habermas thus arrives at the conclusion that our only "utopian" aspirations should be universal formal ones. There must be no "substantive" novelty for this revised philosophy of modernity. "The utopian content of the communications community," Habermas declares "shrinks to the formal aspect of an undamaged intersubjectivity. Even the expression 'ideal speech situation' leads to error in so far as it suggests a concrete way of life."[13] We are free when we have no other master than our reason, and it is now that master that requires us to renounce any substantive utopia, any hope that there might be something *after* "modernity."

Rorty wants to have a master who says there is no master, solidarity with what holds solidarity to be only a contingent affair. He wants the lack of philosophical mastery to itself be a tradition we can all come to agree upon. His "liberal utopia" is the world populated only by democratic ironists. What is new for the populace of this utopia is always only a matter of private pastime; for what can happen in public has been settled in advance by the bloodless agreement that founds the utopia. John Dewey is a founding father of this utopian constitution, and America its place of origin.

Of the three, it is thus Foucault alone who holds out for substantive novelty in the public practices of critical thought. For Foucault, the lack of mastery is not an ironical stance circumscribed by a tradition we must first agree upon. It is rather found in those problematizing moments in the specific traditions in which we find ourselves, that opens them to unforeseen possibilities—the "events" through which we become something other than what we have been, and so ask us who we are today. The problem of novelty is the problem of such moments of "transcendence."

For Habermas, the problem with the "transcendental turn" in philosophy has been that it imagined transcendence in the image of a subject. The only way out is to model it instead on the "undamaged intersubjectivity" presupposed by any rational communication. Rorty would have us abandon the idea of transcendence altogether. For Foucault, there is a transcendence that is not that of a subject, or of a universal framework of discourse, but rather that of the events in the particular discourses of which we are capable at a time and place. Such transcendence is thus not ideal and timeless but material and ever-changing. It is the "it poses itself" of a question in the midst of the assumptions upon which our knowledge, our procedures, our agreements rest. It is this moment of the lack of philosophical mastery or "self-assurance" that is creative of new possibilities, of which we do not yet possess the image. And this transcendence, prior to agreed norms, which initiates without founding, is the chance and the risk of our freedom. Critical enlightenment should thus proceed in as many directions as there arise such new questions, such new possibilities.

There is then a renewed *political* question of our time to which these three revisions in critical thought may be read as a response. Basic to the immediate political past from which we seem to be emerging are what Foucault at one point calls the "diseases of power," Stalinism and Fascism. A revived philosophical discussion of democracy corresponds to a crisis in the practice of philosophical critique which these two diseases expose. That is something which all three philosophers cannot help but confront.

In conformity with their views of critical thought, Habermas, and in a rather more complacent way, Rorty, attempt to identify with those political ideologies that stood in opposition to such diseases of power, and to show how to argue against those ideologies which did not. There is a search for an identity between their philosophies and those ideologies that secured or promoted democratic government. There is thus the sense that there will be no secure democracy without a universal pragmatics of speech, or without the ironies of liberal conversation.

In conformity with his philosophy, Foucault starts in another way. Suspending prior ideological identification, he proposed to analyze the specific ways these two "diseases" formed part of the complex history of our own political experience. His conjecture was that the failure of Stalinism and Fascism as ideologies of global social transformation helped to expose the workings of the "political technologies" on which they relied—concrete practices or procedures for governing ourselves and one another. From this point of view, he argued, Stalinism and Fascism were not so original. They used and extended techniques of our own still existing sorts of political rationality. It was then by identifying this rationality of our own techniques for governing ourselves that we might analyze just how an ideology such as liberalism had tried to restrict their excesses and why it did not succeed. Instead of starting with "solidarity" with an existing democratic ideology, and asking history to explain what prevented people in the past from adopting it, Foucault may thus be said to have made of democracy, not a source of retrospective identification, but a *question* for our current ways of governing ourselves and organizing our societies.

It is thus Foucault's kind of critical philosophy that would allow us to see in democracy not only an actual program of government, but also a form of resistance to the eternalization or essentialization of the ways of governing we have so far invented for ourselves. As distinct from a democratic policy or rule, there would thus be the *question* of democracy—a space of critical questioning which no government could ever completely regulate or silence. Such would be the space of freedom which Foucault terms the "permanent provocation" in any form of power.

And, it is precisely this priority of the *question* (of democracy) with respect to existing policies of government which was, for Foucault, the political originality of '68. Then a host of new questions started to be asked ("about women, about relations between the sexes, about medicine, about mental illness, about the environment, about minorities, about delinquency").[14] They were questions for which a *definitive* solution seemed neither possible nor desirable. They were questions posed *to* Marxism rather than ones that sought a preexisting solution in Marxism, questions that would have caused Marxism to transform itself, to the point of introducing a "crisis" in it. There was in short "a plurality of questions posed to politics rather than the reinscription of the act of questioning in the framework of a political doctrine."[15] And it was this disengagement of the act of questioning from existing doctrine as to how to govern ourselves, in which Foucault sought a new sort of "citizenship" for critical thought.

> The work of an intellectual is not to mold the political will of others, it is, through the analyses that he does in his own field, to reexamine evidence and assumptions, to shake up habitual ways of working and thinking, to dissipate conventional familiarities, to reevaluate rules and institutions, and starting from this reproblematization (where he occupies his specific profession as an intellectual) to participate in the formation of a political will (where he has his role as citizen to play).[16]

There are then two features of the question of democracy that might be associated with Foucault's practice of the question of enlightenment. In the first place, we must raise the question of democracy not simply from a formal point of view, or in terms of the procedures of practical reason, but from a "pragmatic" point of view, or in terms of this "world" not of what we are meant to be, but in which we make ourselves and in which who we are can become a question for our free invention. And in the second place, we must recognize that the question of democracy has as rich and complex a history as the question of enlightenment, forming a part of our most *actuel passé*. Moreover the two questions are interconnected. Just as the question of enlightenment is not that of a past period of our history, but of a relation *to* our history that survives the formulations we give to it, so the question of democracy is not that of an inherited form of government, but of a relation *to* government that survives the solutions we find for it. That is why democracy like enlightenment is not the end of history, but its constant recommencement.

When Foucault says an intellectual today is not someone with a definitive political theory, but someone who helps raise questions *to* politics, he may thus be said to state a principle of "the question of democracy." The principle says there may be no theory to decide in advance what to do when people come to question what is legitimate or illegitimate, in their social arrangements; what is tolerable or intolerable, in their lives. It says that when such questioning arises, it is rather new spaces of critical thought and action which we must invent in the absence of a master—philosophical or governmental. The role of the intellectual would be to help to create and to articulate such "democratic" spaces of the question, spaces of which he is not himself the master.

In this way we come back to the problem of new philosophies, and, in particular, to the creative situation when the language into which we must translate something is as yet unspoken and never completely understood. Perhaps the practice of "the question" in philosophy is this pragmatism in critical thought which is translation without a master.

NOTES

1. Habermas, *The Philosophical Discourse of Modernity* (Cambridge: MIT Press, 1987), p. 183.

2. *Ibid.*, p. 192.

3. A longer, more detailed and more critical reading of Habermas is to be found in "Habermas' Complaint" below.

4. Habermas, *The Philosophical Discourse of Modernity*, p. 206.

5. Foucault's thesis may be consulted at the library of the University of Paris.

6. Foucault, *Technologies of the Self*, Martin, Gutman, Hutton, eds. (Amherst: University of Massachusetts Press, 1988).

7. Foucault, Introduction to Georges Canguilhem, *The Normal and the Pathological* (New York: Zone, 1989), p. 10.

8. *Ibid.*, p. 9.

9. *The Foucault Reader*, Rabinow, ed. (New York: Pantheon, 1984), p. 46.

10. *Ibid.*, p. 385.

11. *Ibid.*

12. "The Subject and Power" in *Michel Foucault: Beyond Structuralism and Hermeneutics*, Dreyfus and Rabinow (Chicago: University of Chicago Press, 1982), p. 211.

13. Habermas, "The New Obscurity," in *Philosophy and Social Criticism* (Winter 1986), vol. 2, no. 2.

14. *The Foucault Reader*, p. 386.

15. *Ibid.*

16. "The Concern for Truth," in *Foucault Live* (Semiotext (e) 1989), pp. 305–306.

TWO

Habermas' Complaint

THE PHOBIA OF IRRATIONALITY

In the twelve lectures and five excurses that comprise *The Philosophical Discourse of Modernity*, Jürgen Habermas takes on the "neostructuralists," whom he sees as his rivals, in a combative, impassioned, often acrimonious spirit. He admonishes them; he lectures them; he caricatures and ridicules them. He will redress the dangerous error at the heart of their work. All this assumes epic proportions. Nothing less than the entire history of modern philosophy since Kant is at issue. And, for Habermas, that means the entire history of modern society since the Enlightenment.

In a polemic of this sort, fueled by an unstated grievance, one is placed in a position of trying to locate the source of the complaint. I suspect that Habermas' complaint comes from a fear of the consequences—real or imagined—of the poststructuralist questioning of our history. I think that what Habermas fears in this questioning is the possibility of an anti-democratic irrationalism. Since it seems to me that this fear is a misplaced one, I call it Habermas' "phobia

This article originally appeared in *New German Critique* (Fall 1988), 45:163–191. Reprinted here with permission of the editors.

of irrationality," and I conjecture that it has its roots in the historical experience of National Socialism. Habermas, the champion of undistorted dialogue and undamaged intersubjectivity, grew up in the Hitler Youth movement. His first philosophical interest and greatest philosophical disappointment was with Heidegger. The student movements of the '60s at first inspired in him a fear of "red fascism."

Foucault and Derrida, within three years Habermas' contemporaries, spent their formative war years not in Germany but in German-occupied France and French North Africa.[1] There was no Hitler Youth, and eventually a different attitude to Heidegger. At about the time of Habermas' disappointment with Heidegger, Foucault was quitting the French Communist Party, which, in those years, had banned the work of Heidegger. He quit before Hungary in 1956, and the reason he gave did not have to do with "irrationalism" but with the sort of "hyperrationality" of Soviet science; his research into the institutions of psychiatric knowledge coincided with the Lysenko affair. By his own account, he then sought a way out of the phenomenology and Marxism that dominated the thought of the period. On this score, Derrida's story is rather different. But both Derrida and Foucault, who, in the '60s had an exchange of their own, found that their respective work had acquired, with the events of 1968 in Paris, an unanticipated actuality or modernity.

These elementary biographical facts gain significance in the larger frame of the philosophical war Habermas now declares on his Parisian contemporaries, and helps to explain why even mutual acquaintance between these major partners in "Continental philosophy" and critical thought should occur so late in their development and assume the form of a confrontation. For, in fact, there is common ground; these philosophers may have more important enemies than each other. There is a common sense of a crisis in the very conception of the left intellectual, and, connected with it, an importance attributed, even if in different ways, to the political innovations of the postwar "social movements" that shook the university and for which '68 is a symbolic date. But Habermas' polemic brings something else to the fore. It is as though the anamnesis of the War, its unspeakable brutalities and its death camps, its complicities and its resistances, as well as the consequences of its settlement, have become after the fact, a central question for the tradition of historically minded critical thought: that is what now seems to at once divide and draw together these philosophers whose formative years were spent when their respective nations were locked in a cataclysmic world war. The problem of "modernity," which is the central theme of Habermas' book, may be regarded as the problem, within this framework, of the connection of philosophy to *history* in the conception of its intellectual tasks.

READINGS

In this book Habermas is reading for the first time, in any extended manner, work which for the most part appeared in French almost twenty years ago, and which, in the meantime, has become rather well known in America. One can observe that none of the secondary literature with which Habermas sometimes misleadingly interlaces his presentation of the French authors are from the French; they are all American or German. In Habermas' story of the travels of modern philosophy from Jena via Frankfurt to Paris, one often wonders whether Habermas ever really gets there. From his lectures one learns as much about the German reception of the French thinkers as about the thinkers themselves.

Regarded as an intellectual history of postwar French philosophy, his discussion leaves much to be desired. In this book on neostructuralism, there is practically nothing about structuralism. In this history of social or political theory, there is not a word about Althusser. There is nothing about the questions of sexuality, the body, language, and gender, which made the work of "the neostructuralists" seem important to feminists.

As a historical matter, the label itself is questionable: "neostructuralism" is not nearly so unified or uniform a thing as Habermas imagines. It is not clear precisely whom it groups. Althusser is out, but what about Deleuze or Canguilhem, Kristeva or Blanchot, Lacan or Bourdieu? Does it refer to a common "period" or portion of the work of these figures, or to everything they wrote?

The two figures Habermas does discuss, Foucault and Derrida, thought they had rather basic disagreements with each other. Many people admire one but not the other, and so find their association an unwarranted amalgamation. In any case, "neostructuralism" or "poststructuralism" may not be the best label for what they share, and is not something they ever called themselves.

In particular, it is not clear that "the neostructuralists" have, or would have, just the same view about the central question Habermas raises: the problem of a society providing a justification and a sense of unity for itself without reference to tradition. For it is not

26

a question they explicitly raise. Habermas does not seem to realize that he must first show that they were responding to a question they didn't realize they were asking, before showing that they failed to answer it.

Habermas says he must oversimplify.[2] In this oversimplification he seems to overlook an elementary hermeneutic principle: the work of a philosopher can survive the "context" in which it was formulated and be taken up and transformed in new ways. For, on the one hand, he pays no attention to the "context" in which he himself is reading the work of the neostructuralists. This leads him to regrettable and misguided views. For example, he says that the neostructualists are structural neoconservatives (i.e., neo- two things which don't have much in common). No doubt he has in mind the way the views of the French thinkers seem to him to be similar to those held by German neoconservatives. American neoconservatives would of course agree with most of what Habermas says about the "irrationalism" of the French authors.

On the other hand, Habermas loads the hermeneutic tables by making the French derive from German precursors they are not allowed to read in their own way. Habermas' own rather questionable readings of the other figures in the tradition, Kant, Hegel, Husserl, Heidegger, and Nietzsche, are *not* the readings of the same figures offered by the French philosophers. Habermas is at pains to show that Foucault and Derrida are not the start of something new, but the ending of something they didn't start. "Derrida means to go beyond Heidegger; fortunately he goes back behind him." Foucault's "ingenious" discussion of the "anthropological slumbers" of post-Kantian thought was "already analyzed by Schiller, Fichte, Schelling and Hegel in a similar fashion."[3]

The effect of this dual operation is to fit everything back into a more familiar story of the progression of German philosophy after Kant: the story in which the question of the *Aufklärung* and the "German path to modernity" were linked to one another; the story of the thinking which made an "essentialist" history essential to philosophy, and so made a "discourse" about its own "modernity" central to it.

THE STORY

Habermas' version of this story assumes the form of a counterfactual lament about what could have, and should have, happened in post-Kantian German philosophy, but did not: a rationalist or transcendental embrace of liberal principles.

Apparently reversing an earlier impression, Richard Rorty says he is now convinced by Habermas' "dramatic narrative" even if it is circular or question-begging as a formal argument.[4] I think the "circle" in question lies in the way, in Habermas' narrative, the problem of the "self-assurance" of modernity is interconnected with the self-assurance of Habermas' solution to it. In Habermas' tale we are told that the age or the society we live in is the same one Hegel described when he said that the task of philosophy was to provide a "self-assurance of modernity." When Hegel said a modern society is one that divides up its "value-spheres" according to the topics of Kant's three Critiques, and raised the question of the unity or "civic totality" that stood behind its "diremptions," he set the agenda for the next two centuries of thought. The rest of philosophy consists in various "roads" taken out of nineteenth-century Idealism by the great thinkers of at least the "Continental" part of the philosophy curriculum. Each thinker takes one and only one road; the unity of his thought is given in the way he responds, or fails to respond, to the great question of how a modern society can reassure itself, having lost its traditional sense of unity.

Habermas, however, is not content to trace only the actual roads thus taken by modern philosophers. He also speaks of "crossroads." These are the occasions when a thinker might have taken another road that leads to Habermas' own views on communicative action. His intention, he says, is "to examine once again the directions once suggested at the chief crossroads ... the places where the young Hegel, the young Marx, and even the Heidegger of *Being and Time* and Derrida in his discussion with Husserl, stood before alternative paths they did *not* choose."[5] Thus there are possible as well as actual roads in modern philosophy, and while it was always possible to have taken the Habermasian road, in fact all the actual ones turn out to be dead ends. The law of Habermas' narrative is that while all the actual roads in modern philosophy lead nowhere, all the possible ones lead to him. Thus we find out how to finish what Hegel left unfinished.

Habermas' "dramatic narrative" turns on a distinction between two kinds, or two conceptions, of "reason": the "subject-centered" kind and the "intersubjective" kind, or the "we" of absolute spirit, and the "we" of rational consensus. "Intersubjective" reason consists in the acceptance of rational procedures of communicating.

"Subject-centered" reason is found not simply in the attempt to base reason in a theory of "consciousness," but when it is thought that there exists some absolute "subject" that alienates, or produces, or realizes, itself in history or society. "Undamaged intersubjectivity" serves in Habermas' story as a sort of *deus ex machina* to resolve, retrospectively at least, all the problems into which the "subject-centered" sort of reason would have plunged the philosophical discourse on modernity.

The "philosophical discourse of modernity" thus turns out to be a strange sort of discourse. Everyone who takes it up (i.e., everyone) ends in error, self-contradiction, and "exhaustion"; and yet everyone *might* have found the correct Habermasian solution. The upshot of Habermas' tale of modern philosophy is a sense of a vast intellectual failure we might have spared ourselves had we looked for the timeless presuppositions and aspirations of rational consensus, and derived from them a "grounding" of the wordy version of social democracy Rorty thinks is identical to what Americans call "liberalism." But it is not too late for what should have happened in modern philosophy. Looking back at the errors of the tradition as an edifying exercise, we can at last do what we always should have done.

Reading this "reconstruction" of the last two centuries of philosophical thought, one may well wonder *why* it is that the right road that might always have been taken in fact never was, *why* so many self-defeating philosophies took hold, *why* there was such a constant blindness to the liberal solution to the problem of modernity that was constantly available. Since Habermas keeps the conception of modern society and its problems constant, and looks only at the various philosophical solutions to them, the explanatory part of his history remains somewhat puzzling. His is a purely intellectual, even Idealist history; one learns little of the developments in society that might have been linked to the various philosophical errors. Habermas remains as ever an unreconstructed sociological Idealist. One senses that his story is not offered as an explanation but as a sort of negative demonstration—what happens when one does not take the right road. As such it is a form of self-reassurance by demonstration of the dire consequences of all alternatives.

There is an obvious comfort in this kind of historical demonstration: one can always sort out, after the fact at least, the bad antimodernist "irrationalist" tendencies or "potentials" from the good, progressive, enlightened ones; one can rescue a "core of rationality" from the tradition in spite of all its errors. This is what Habermas, updating Horkheimer and Adorno, calls "the dialectic of the Enlightenment." And it is this philosophical reassurance about modernity that Habermas then brings to his reading of the French neostructuralists. He sees in their work the apotheosis of the bad irrationalist tendencies one needs now to excise from the traditions of German philosophy. While the ostensive topic of Habermas' book is the "French path to postmodernity," a more basic concern seems to be why German philosophy after Kant assumed anti-modern, anti-democratic, "irrationalist" forms. The French authors are only really a belated repetition of the bad elements in German philosophy. Indeed the gist of Habermas' criticism of the neostructuralists is first found in his objections to Adorno.[6]

THE ARGUMENT

This historical charge of the "irrationalism" of the French as latter-day German Romantics is combined with a logical one. Neostructuralism is not only the avatar of a dangerous tradition; it is self-defeating. When it is not historicist, Habermas' objection to his French contemporaries is a meta-objection. He doesn't dispute what they say but the contradiction of their saying it. Their work is riddled with "self-referential paradox"; they are the victims of "performative contradiction." Habermas' polemic thus turns on the question of what a critical philosophical "argument" is.

In this part of his complaint, Habermas runs together two things which Foucault was concerned to distinguish: "irrationality" and "philosophical irrationalism." It was Foucault's idea that irrationality is something that has a history; it is, at least in part, something which is historically (and "rationally") conceived and constructed. To conceive of "madness" as otherworldly marvel, or as "dazzled reason" is not the same as to conceive of it as an individual mental abnormality or deviancy. It is important to look at these changes, their historical conditions and consequences. For the real danger we face may be not so much irrationality as the instituted ways of thinking which conceptualize it, take it as an object, and oblige us to deal with it in a certain way:

"The rationality of the abominable is a fact of contemporary history. The irrational does not thereby acquire unalienable rights ... to respect rationalism as an ideal should never constitute a blackmail to prevent the analysis of the rationalities really at work."[7]

Distinct from the historical construction of "the irrational" is the philosophical view that basic changes and patterns of development in theory or discourse are not governed by rules that were, or could have been, specified in advance, or that these changes do not lead to a single Truth. Such philosophical "irrationalism" is not opposed to Reason but to the "rationalist" conception of it.

Habermas has a neo-Kantian conception of reason, as divided into fixed "spheres," and guided by a priori rules. But one can question this view without being a German Romantic. There exist philosophers who specialize in "grounding validity claims" who don't share Habermas' social views, and those who share his social views who don't do meta-ethics, or who, like Richard Rorty, don't believe in it, thinking "grounding" is a wheel that plays no part in the mechanism. There are even practitioners of rational philosophical argument like Bernard Williams who try to show that the sort of normative theory Habermas thinks modern societies must have to reassure themselves is neither possible nor desirable. To entertain doubts about "grounding modernity out of itself" through a transcendental account of reason, is thus not in itself to thirst for the irrational.

In his phobia, Habermas conflates the irrational with philosophical irrationalism. It is as if the "irrationality" of the fear of the Jews were not a complex historical construct, but the result of the irrationalism of those philosophers who had some doubts about the existence of timeless standards of Reason. This conflation leads Habermas to the fervent conviction that the only way to secure ourselves against a recurrence of fascism is by an unconditional commitment to a universalist rationalist philosophy; whereas, in fact, of course, there were neo-Kantian philosophers and Lutheran ministers to embrace National Socialism along with Heidegger. The dichotomy rationality/irrationality may thus not be the best way of describing the difference between the styles of critical philosophical argument practiced by Habermas and by Foucault or Derrida.

Habermas' quarrel with the neostructuralists is not the first of its kind. Previously he took on Gadamer, Luhmann, and his mentor, Adorno. In each case there is the need to formulate a line to be unanimously repeated by all "rational" agents. In each case there is the idea that to "argue" philosophically is to specify or to appeal to a principle or ideal which would unambiguously regulate the argument.

31

In Derrida and Foucault (and even in their controversy with each other) there is another conception of philosophical argument: to argue is to open thinking by exposing something unthought in it. The "genealogical critique" of Foucault and the "deconstructive questioning" of Derrida are not rationalist styles of argument; and yet they are not assaults on Reason itself. In neither case are they arguments *for* "irrationality." They do not promote a Rousseauistic or Romantic authenticity of an irrational spirituality. They are, in their own ways, as critical of such Romanticism as is Habermas. (Habermas is mistaken in picturing *Madness and Civilization* as a Romantic search for a "new mythology" of the irrational). And yet they involve a style of critique and a kind of questioning which do not assume the form of a judgment by reference to incontestable principles or suppose a single procedure to settle all disagreements.

Their question is not that of an anxiety or uncertainty about the possibility of rational normative justification it would be the sole business of philosophy to overcome. It is more a matter of *injecting* a little anxiety or uncertainty in forms of action, thought, or expertise that operate unquestionably with routine self-evidence. It is concerned with a sort of "skepticism" about what is taken for granted in the ways we go about things.

These styles of argument involve a particular conception of the connection between philosophy and history, which is different from the one Habermas takes for granted. In promoting a "rationalist" concept of reason, Habermas thinks that the first task of the intellectual is to locate the institution of those values or norms from which no enlightened person could dissent, values which are as independent of change and history as possible, and which can thus serve as standards of critical judgment. Philosophical argument in Foucault and Derrida moves in another direction or has another aim. There is a kind of critique and a kind of questioning which would respond to those events which are happening to us, in us, around us, but which we do not yet know how to conceive or judge, which raise questions about who we are in the present moment. Thus they understand critical "modernity" not as an *acquisition* of timeless norms of reason to be defended against all deviations, but as *event*, as critical opening of new possibilities in our thinking. This difference in the conception of modernity recurs in Habermas' objections to Foucault's "positivism" and Derrida's "aestheticism."

FOUCAULT'S POSITIVISM

For Foucault the crisis of historically minded critical philosophy was a crisis in the sort of grand history which was propounded by Hegel, and which Habermas would continue, for example, in what he calls Evolutions-theory. Foucault thought we might now see the *Aufklärung* not as a discovery of an incontestable "adequate description" of our society as a whole, but as an "event" that made the question of its own history basic to the critical task of philosophy. He thought that offering-adequate-descriptions-of-society-as-a-whole-with-a-view-to-a-general-critique was just what was being problematized and transformed in this tradition of philosophical critique. It is by reference to this "event" that he tried to create his own style of historical criticism.

Thus, in Kant's short paper "What Is Enlightenment?" of 1784, Foucault saw the beginnings of a tradition in philosophy concerned with the critical question of who we are today, or in our "modernity," a question which would have been formulated and transformed in different ways in France, Germany, and the Anglo-Saxon countries. "Europe, for soon nearly two centuries, has entertained an extremely rich and complex relation with this event of the *Aufklärung* about which Kant and Mendelsohn were already reflecting in 1784. This relation has not stopped transforming itself without ever effacing itself. The *Aufklärung* is, to use an expression of G. Canguilhem, our most *actuel passé*."[8]

The immediate successors to Kant had turned the event of the *Aufklärung* into "the moment in which philosophy found the possibility of constituting itself as the determinant figure of an epoch, and in which that epoch became the form of completion of the philosphy."[9] The question of the present moment became a question from which philosophy could not separate itself; history became one of the central problems of philosphy.

But the question of "modernity" need not be formulated as a question about the constitutive features of the modern period; perhaps that sort of grand theory is no longer possible for philosophy. One can conceive of modernity instead as an attitude toward the events that silently form the history in which one finds oneself. There arises the possibility of a form of critique "that will not seek to identify the universal structure of all knowledge or all possible action, but will seek the instances of discourse that articulate what we think, say and do as so many historical events."[10]

For this sort of critical intelligence, "history" would be what delimits and restricts who we are and may be, and "modernity" those events which change this, or through which we become something other than we are. "Modernity" thus involves a critical attitude to history, which does not consist in thinking that things are, or are not, moving in the right direction, but that they might be otherwise than they are. One must be constantly alive to what has not been noticed is transpiring in our *passé actuel.* One no longer searches for the point of progression of society to a wholly enlightened state, but tries to expose what we take for granted as necessary and fixed in our existence as something that has been happening to us, and which we may refuse to accept. The critical aim of his work, said Foucault, was to "eventalize history": to inject a sense of possibility and event just where people see only something unchanging in the ways they think and go about things, and to respond to the "problematizations" that open those ways of thinking to the possibility of change and transformation. In this way, he would show that "we are not, and do not have to place ourselves, under the sign of a unique necessity."[11]

This critical historical attitude is already found in the discussion of "events" in history, which introduces the *Archeology of Knowledge.* Canguilhem and Bachelard initiated a tradition which sought to introduce events into the received picture of science as a unified cumulative enterprise (that is how they reformulated the question of Enlightenment, or of the history of reason). Foucault argued that this tradition was thus connected to the "new history" that descends from the *Annales* School. This School had also brought a new class of "events" into the field of history—such things as price cycles, demographic trends, climatic changes, technological innovations of a "material civilization." The more such things were seen to have a history, the more it became difficult to advance a unified history for all things. The sort of "total history" which unifies events "around a single centre—principle, a meaning, a spirit, a world-view, an overall shape" was being replaced by a "general history" concerned with the "space of dispersion" of events.[12]

Foucault said that "the event" of these new histories was to be found in a common break with the teleology and anthropologism of nineteenth-century historicism—with the idea of History as the self-realization of some absolute entity such as Man. The task of history was thus no longer to "memorialize" the past but to "even-

talize" it: to rediscover the events in the mass of "material docu-
mentation" with which a society is always "inextricably linked."
Foucault's own "archeology" of the "events of discourse" would be
made possible by this event in the study of history: it would turn
to those anonymous events in our thinking which form our *passé
actuel.*

Our "rich and complex relation" with the *Aufklärung* had therefore undergone a number of transformations. The question of modernity has been formulated in different ways and in different
places. The *philosophical* question of who we are today has not
been committed to a single fixed *historical* view of modern society.
Rather the philosophical discourse *of* modernity has changed with
the transformations in the historical discourse *on* modernity. That
is why we today can no longer simply recycle the historical model
of modern society proposed by the immediate successors to Kant,
but must take up the question in a different way and in altered
circumstances. In particular, Foucault thought that by introducing
"events" into their fields, the new history of science and the new
history of society helped to change the way the Enlightenment
question was formulated.

Habermas is not much impressed by the "philosophical" significance of the new history of science. He introduces his lecture on
Foucault by declaring that Foucault worked out his irrationalist
impulses ". . . not as a philosopher, but as a student of Bachelard,
and even as a historian of science."[13] But Bachelard and Foucault
were not alone in thinking that the history of science might deci-
sively transform the philosophical conception of it. It would correct
the deficiencies of an ahistorical epistemology; it would offer a
better way of thinking of the "rationality" of the sciences than the
possession of a single timeless method of appraisal, or a fixed
relation between representation and reality. The "rationality" of
science is not a single monolithic thing; the objectivity of a science
would be properly seen in terms of its patterns of development.
Motivating such research was not a Romantic yearning for the
irrational but an attempt to offer a better account of "rationality".
In particular it sought to offer a better account of the "history of
reason" than the one which identified that history with a global
"modernity" of societies.[14]

In the "French" tradition of Bachelard, Canguilhem (Koyré, Du-
hem, and many others) one finds an investigation of the supposed
"modernity" of modern science more complex, more precise, and

more closely supported by actual research than anything in the *Dialectic of the Enlightenment*. The more the actual formation and transformation of domains of science were investigated, the more difficult it became to maintain the idea of a single great "revolution" that would separate modern empirical investigation from myth, superstition, and speculation; the more difficult it became to analyze the "external" social factors in the development of the sciences in terms of a general "philosophical" social theory dividing ancient from modern societies. Habermas notes in passing that Foucault did not derive his account of the "classical order" in the *Order of Things* from received ideas about the "mathematization of nature," but he doesn't seem to realize that this was a more general strategy in his work: through a new analysis of specific episodes to expose the inadequacies of received "philosophical" accounts of a general "modernity" in all the sciences.

But the great socio-historical "moment" of modernity was also questioned through the new social history. The introduction of new objects into social history transformed the general "periodizations" that had been formulated by the Romantic and Idealist "philosophical discourse of modernity." As the body, death, deviancy, family life, climate, race, gender, forms of writing, technologies of dissemination, and much else, became objects of specific histories, it became increasingly difficult to think that all might be subsumed under a total history in which "modernity" would figure as a "learning process" on the part of the evolving human species of the *Aufklärung* with its ensuing "dialectics."

Thus Foucault thought a different kind of historical analysis of the exercise of power in modern societies was required than the ones that derive from the great nineteenth-century stories of the growing state domination of society, of modernization, and the rise of the bureaucracy, or of the transition from feudalism to capitalism. He thought one might analyze specific singular "events" in the ways power works in terms of the techniques people devise to govern themselves and one another, and the knowledge and practice on which those techniques depend and which they reinforce. "Discipline" would be one such event in "power-knowledge"; what makes it "modern" would not be given through the traditional contrast between status and contract, or *Gemeinschaft* and *Gesellschaft*.

In Foucault's idiom, a technique of governing is not, in itself, *domination*. It is an "open strategy" in which a particular form of domination becomes possible and in which it can be limited or restricted in particular ways. Foucault thought this offered a better way of thinking about the history of domination than the Romantic one, which understands it basically as turning the warm rich "life-world" into a natural object.

Habermas runs roughshod over these distinctions. He conflates Foucault's conception of "power" with "domination," and "domination" with "reification" or instrumentalizing the lifeworld. Then, in order to generate "self-referential paradox," he attributes to Foucault a "discourse on modernity" according to which there is one and only one "domination" which emcompasses all knowledge and applies to society as a whole. He thus ends up ascribing to Foucault just what Foucault denies: the idea of power as a single and implacable domination so total there is no escape from it; and the idea of critique as a suspicion thus cast on society as a whole.

When Foucault says modern society is a disciplinary one, he is not saying that everything in it is disciplined, but that it introduces a new "strategy of power."[15] He also says modern societies are "medico-confessional," "insurantial" and "bio-political." This doesn't mean that discipline is biopower is confession is insurance, and that all are best analyzed as instrumentalizing the lifeworld, or that there is a single procedural solution to them. The idea of "totality" is not a methodological assumption of Foucault's concept of power; it is part of what he wanted to study. He thought it was an important, and analyzable, feature of biopower or discipline, not that they are total, but that they are totalizing just as they are individualizing. He thought that the constitution of individuality should be analyzed in new ways that did not depend on the sociological opposition between individual and society; he thought there was more to the constitution of the subject than participation in discussion, and that its analysis required other categories than those of reification, or turning subjects into objects.

In Foucault's critical attitude, we thus find a dual operation. On the one hand, Foucault tried to devise an analysis of the history of forms of knowledge which does not start from the "philosophical discourse on modernity," and a style of critical analysis which does not start from a general view about the "modernity" of societies as a whole. On the other hand, he tried to rethink "modernity" not as a general or "unavoidable" property of all knowledge and all society, but as the name of a critical attitude to the specific forms of power which confront us, and help to determine who we are and can be.

Thus what is distinctive about Foucault is that he did *not* derive his critique from a "philosophical discourse on modernity," but tried to question the global assumptions of such a discourse from the standpoint of new problems, forms of analysis, and events. He thought we could now get a better picture of the operations of modern society by reading the annals of public hygiene than by reading Hegel. He offered an example of what it means to *delimit* a problem, analyze it specifically, and use the result to question received "philosophical" conceptions and models of explanation and justification.

Habermas' Germanic misconstrual of this project recurs in his basic criticism of it: the difficulties of its "positivism" and its "cryptonormativism."

Habermas seizes on a passage in *L'Ordre du discours* where Foucault refers to the "felicitous positivism" of the genealogist. By "positivism" Habermas understands the importation of the "objectivizing" or "instrumental" Interest of the natural sciences into "hermeneutical" or "critical" ones. Thus the passages show that Foucault was trying to examine the history of knowledge from the standpoint of the wrong Interest, and so was contradicting himself.

In fact, in the passage in question, Foucault refers to "constituting domains of objects in relation to which one can affirm true or false propositions," and then he says "let us call these domains of objects positivist, and to play on words again, let us say the genealogical mood is one of felicitous positivism."[16]

The humorless Habermas doesn't realize that in this "play on words," Foucault was using "positivism" in a different sense than his own. It concerns what Foucault called the "positivity" of a domain of knowledge. It raises a different question than that of method, or "criteria of validity according to which what is true gets differentiated from what is false." It is not about the "criteria" by which one comes to agree to propositions, but what sorts of propositions, or which domains of objects, there *can* be agreement about. Thus for example, the fact that the pattern of development in a form of knowledge like psychiatry is not commanded by a body of deductive theory does not show it is based on a non-positivist Interest of understanding or demystifying, but that it acquires its objects, or establishes its "positivity," in a particular way, whose conditions and consequences the genealogist is content to study.

Thus we might draw the contrast with Habermas the other way around. On the one hand, Habermas remains a felicitous anti-positivist. He thinks that if we get our kinds of methods straight, we can resolve the questions Foucault raises about cataloguing mental abnormalities or specifying a criminal population: return our activities to their proper "value-spheres" or kinds of "validity-claims"; get our knowledge in line with its proper Interests. On the other hand, Habermas is a deficient positivist, since he thinks that one account of society is "unavoidable"; he thinks there are historical models and assumptions which cannot be contested or "falsified": that modern societies *are* those that divide up their "value-spheres" in a particular manner, or that "irrationalism" always leads in modern societies to fascism.

Habermas' second and related charge is that Foucault's "felicity" in the critical study of the events of knowledge/power commits him to a "cryptonormativism." Foucault's problem would be the reverse of the one contained in the old adage Kant discussed: "this may be true in theory but does it apply in practice?" The practice of his critique would appeal to something which could not be true on his theory. Habermas thus raises a question about the place of values or norms in Foucault's critical history.

Foucault did envisage a form of historical critique that would not be "normative" in the sense that it would not assume the form of a judgment by reference to norms or values independently guaranteed. Rather it would attempt to reconstitute in as "objective" or "positive" (and in this sense as "rational") a way as possible a specific thing people were saying and doing to themselves and to one another, and, in effect, to ask: do we accept it, will we tolerate it, and if not, what might we do about it?

Foucault made a point of refusing the "transference effect" of such a critique—the demand that one provides a definite solution to the critical question one opens in this way. He thought we could identify the problems we face without identifying with universal Humanity, and even without knowing in advance precisely the procedures to discuss and deal with them.

While such a critique does not then base itself in unassailable "normative standards," it would open critical question about our "values" or "norms," and the practices in which they figure. It opens questions about the social and political forms we want, and of which we are capable. In this sense Foucault's "cryptonormativism" is not a concealed judgment of "value," but an attempt to raise questions about the "events" which change the contents of what people take to be "valuable." For Foucault thought that our sense of our "values" was transformed through changes in *actual* discourse and not by reference to the supposedly ideal assumptions of the *act* of discussing them. Thus, the content of "justice" would change in relation to the actual discourses Foucault sought to analyze under the heading of "bio-power," and it is actual changes in discourse, whose history we can examine, which led us to remove "feminine virtue" from the catalogue of Universal Human Values. It is these "events" to which Foucault thought we should pay attention.

It was this kind of critical genealogical investigation of the *invention* of values with which Foucault was concerned in his last work. He was asking the critical question of why, as regards our sexual experience, we today, ethically speaking, are no longer Greek, no longer Christian, but are becoming something else.

DERRIDA'S AESTHETICISM

Out of ignorance or dislike or both combined, Habermas' discussion of Derrida is particularly weak. He refuses to argue with Derrida on the grounds that Derrida refuses to argue. He focuses instead on what Culler says about Searle. He thus fails to confront Derrida on the very episode which links "modernity" to Kantian philosophy which he is attempting to reconstruct step by step. He does not consider that Derrida's early questioning of Rousseauistic ideas about the "origins" of language, and Husserlian ideas about the "origins" of modern "European" science might have something to do with it.

Habermas has two interrelated worries about Derrida: the collapse of the "genre-distinction" between philosophy and literature, and the collapse of all standards of critical judgment into merely "aesthetic" considerations or preferences. But I am not sure that these worries accurately capture Derrida's purposes.

On my own reading at any rate, Derrida was concerned with questioning the ways in which philosophy, in delimiting or defining the "genre" of art (that would belong to a fixed classificatory system of "genres" and "species"), would delimit or define itself, or its own "genre." This questioning has a direct application to the post-Kantian or post-critical "discourse on modernity." For, if that discourse conceived of art as historical, and as an access to History, it conceived of History itself on the model of art. If the *Aufklärung* was the central act of "modernity," "modernity" was conceived, in relation to the ancients, on an "aesthetic" model. Indeed Habermas says as much in his own discussion of "subject-centered reason."

But Derrida, concerned with the question of the "genre" of this kind of philosophical history, uses this fact to offer another reading of Kant than the standard one Habermas accepts, which leads to speculative Idealism. He focuses on the difficult and involuted theme of analogy (and judgment as if . . .) in Kant's Critique, and the theme of the Unity of its three "realms," which, already in the *opus posthumum* points toward Idealism.

This leads Derrida to ask whether the "historicity" (or "modernity") of art can be conceived on another model, or on another relation to models, than the one the third Critique bequeathed to Hegel. He focuses on the "analogism" of the very conception of the "history of art" in the discourse on modernity. In his seminar on Kant of 1974, Derrida says that in introducing a Rousseauistic conception of nature and history "the opposition nature/history would take the analogical relay of *physistechne*," and goes on to say: ". . . if the philosophy of art has always had the greatest difficulty *(le plus grand mal)* in dominating the history of art, or a certain concept of the historicity of art, it is, paradoxically, because it thought art too easily as historical. What I am advancing here naturally supposes the transformation, from one statement to the other, of the concept of history. That will be the work of this seminar . . ."[17]

The question he raised in this way was not that of an irrational "aestheticism" of the grounds of judgment, or of the distinction between philosophy and literature, but of a different conception of the "work" of judgment, historically and politically, as well as philosophically, in its relation to what we still call "art" or literature."

In this light, it is striking to observe that Habermas' own "reconstruction" of the discourse on modernity turns on a sort of "genre-distinction" between the "philosophical" discourse and an "aesthetic" one, from which it would originate through an act of "elevation," and which it has not stopped "touching upon" and "overlapping" in manifold ways. Habermas begins by saying he will not discuss this.

> Since the late eighteenth century modernity has been elevated to a *philosophical* theme in this discourse. The philosophical discourse of modernity touches upon and overlaps with the aes-

thetic discourse in manifold ways. Nevertheless I have had to limit the theme; these lectures do not treat modernism in art and literature.[18]

But this isolation of philosophy from aesthetics in the reconstruction of its constitutive question itself raises a certain number of questions: According to what "criteria" is the "philosophical" distinguished from the "aesthetic" or "literary" discourse on modernity? What is meant by this "elevation" (as when it is said that Hegel was "the first to *raise* to the level of a philosophical problem the process of detaching modernity from the suggestion of norms lying outside itself in the past")?[19] In short, what is the status of "philosophy" in the philosophical discourse of modernity; and what is the status of the "reconstruction" of this discourse and of this "elevation"? To what "genre" does *it* belong? empirical? speculative? literary or philosophical? is it open to question?

Reading Habermas' reconstruction in this light, one discovers that the elevation of philosophy from aesthetics is not so easy as it appears. In fact, in its ascent, the discourse on modernity only finally reaches "philosophy" when it raises itself all the way up to the level of Habermas. For, while Hegel elevated what started out as an aesthetic discourse about the necessity of a new or modern culture to the level of social theory, in Hegel, and then in Marx, the aesthetic or Romantic origins of the discourse are secretly preserved through the model of "subject-centered reason." History is still seen as the self-realization of a "subject," as though it were the work of a Romantic genius.

According to Habermas, at first, Hegel, like Hölderlin and Schelling, offered a "mythopoetic" solution to the anxiety or need for a modern totality. Then he raised the problem to social theory. Hegel "integrates, as it were, the opposition between modernity and antiquity found in the theory of art into a theory of society."[20] The result is the first "conceptual framework" that is "terminologically adequate to modern society."

But, in elevating the Romantic need for unification to the *Wissenschaft* of social theory, he didn't raise it up far enough. His *Wissenschaft* remains contaminated with aestheticism. At the very moment Hegel invents the "genre" of speculative Idealism, he smuggles in the scheme of the self-return of the Absolute; and this deprives his "social theory" of its proper "scientific" or "rational" status. The same concealed aestheticism infects the sort of "praxis philosophy" propounded by Lukačs. For Marx too "smuggled into his concept of praxis" "the aesthetic experience that springs from Romantic art."[21]

This "aesthetic" element is overcome only with the philosophy of "undamaged intersubjectivity" which Hegel and Marx could have and should have advanced but did not. The great aesthetic problem of the moderns and the ancient receives its "philosophical" resolution only when it is absorbed and elevated into a realm or a kind of communication which does not depend on it: a procedure of judgment from which the "aesthetic question" had been eliminated or subordinated.

Thus Habermas' "genre-distinction" between literature and philosophy depends on the existence of "an intersubjective communication" in which art or aesthetic judgment no longer has a determinant place, but in which one can sort out the rational core of the "community" or "civic totality" to which the Romantics aspired in linking art, history, and critical theory into a discourse on modernity. That core consists in the "communications, community-building and solidarity-giving force of art, which is to say, its *public character*."[22] Community-building and solidarity-giving would no longer be understood in terms of the force of art, but the force of art in terms of the communicational solidarity of reason. For Habermas the "motivation behind German Idealism" was to find a substitute or equivalent for God, to ask "whether the social integrative powers of the religious tradition shaken by the Enlightenment can find an equivalent in the unifying, consensus creating power of Reason."[23] But one must replace the aesthetic, literary conception of this rational equivalent with a liberal communicational one. At the heart of Habermas' genre distinction is thus the problem of overcoming Romanticism in a rational "determinant negation."

Habermas' belated self-elevation out of Romanticism thus preserves the Romantic *problem* or question of modernity: "the anxiety caused by the fact that a modernity without models has to stabilize itself on the basis of the very diremptions (or questions, *Entzweiungen*) it wrought,"[24] or again, the problem of the "need for unification." Habermas' "philosophical" solution to this anxiety or need is to rethink the problem of a modern "civic totality" in terms of the conditions of ideal speech.

But to accept as a starting point the Romantic need for a "modern myth," or for imitating the ancients without imitating their cultural or social models, is to rule out other readings for which the attempt to find a modern substitute or equivalent for the lost "totality" or "unity" of the ancient *polis* or the Christian community, would be something of an invented problem, and not so unavoidable as Habermas assumes.

One might after all wonder whether the very ideas of "myth" and "total community" and "the formation of the human race to freedom" are not themselves something of a retrospective "invention" (to use the phrase of Marcel Detienne),[25] the outcome of a style of thought of a particular time and place. One might see the great German *angst* or lack of "self-reassurance" as more the *product* of the "discourse on modernity" than its *origin*. Instead of taking the "totality" that would precede the "diremptions" of modernity as a question it is the sole task of "philosophy" to formulate in a new and non-aesthetic way, one might ask whether it is not itself a sort of myth, which is after all not so modern, with anticipations or roots within the tradition. In this way one might start to "deconstruct" rather than to "reconstruct" the philosophical discourse on modernity advanced by the immediate successors to Kant, where, of course, this is distinct from being "against" all modern forms of life.

This sort of questioning is pursued by Derrida's students Philippe Lacoue-Labarthe and Jean-Luc Nancy in their commentary of the Jena Romantics in *The Literary Absolute* of 1978.[26] There is a different reading of the very material Habermas discusses in his opening lectures where he defines the central question of modern philosophy. The question of the role of "critical theory" in avant-garde art, or in the "aesthetic discourse of modernity" is read in a different way from Habermas' scheme of its elevation and absorption into sociology and consensus "philosophy" as well as the scheme of the "autonomous work" and the "lifeworld" proposed by Peter Bürger.

Perhaps one might put the difference in this way. What Habermas analyzes as "subject-centered reason," Lacoue-Labarthe and Nancy discuss as the scheme of the "literary absolute," in which an absolute, or indivisible entity, or "subject," would critically reproduce itself in culture. The stress is thus placed not on "reason" but on the concept of work (oeuvre, *ergon*) in the self-production of the absolute. With this conception the question of Kant's "analogism" comes into play: the way it helps preserve the link between *physis* and *techné* in the very moment through which it would critically distinguish itself from the ancients. Confronting the historicity of the literary absolute would thus not be a form of "reason" from which the question of literature had been purged, but another way of conceiving of the role of critical judgment in the conception of art and its "historicity" or modernity, a way the authors associate with Maurice Blanchot's idea of *désoeuvrement*. Thus they find another role for Hölderlin's "interruption" of the literary absolute, and for the theme of the sublime in Kant.

In this way they raise the question of a "community" (and therefore a "politics") of art which would not be based on the model of the self-production or self-realization of a human essence (found in both the aesthetic and philosophical genres of the discourse on modernity), but would not have recourse to a conception of intersubjectivity "undamaged" by the question of representation. They associate such community instead with a form of critical judgment which is concerned not with rational consensus, but with the sort of "dissensus" which opens new possibilities, and with a "responsibility" to the modernity of those events through which it occurs.

It is the question not of the "communications community," but of the "literary community."[27] It is in terms of this question that they would rethink the "history of the avant-garde."

A LEARNING EXPERIENCE

Habermas' book inadvertently illustrates what his philosophy denies. It shows how philosophical "communication" can come not from undamaged intersubjectivity and the aspirations for rational consensus, but from dissension, misunderstanding, and incommensurability. For it is just in its misunderstandings that his book raises the most interesting questions about his own work as well as about the work he is attempting to disqualify.

One need not stray far from "liberalism" to recognize that there exist forms of philosophical exchange that are "open" not in the sense that one party must vanquish the other with the "better argument" (or disqualify him by showing to a third party that he has unwittingly failed to observe the rules that make all "rational" discussion possible) but simply in the sense that the outcome is not given in advance. There are after all situations where differences exist over the way an argument is to be framed so as to provide for possible agreement, and they are often philosophically the most fruitful ones. Such situations require a "learning experience," which is perhaps more modest than that of a society as a whole, and for which perhaps after all Nietzsche may provide a better model than Piaget's account of the child's acquisition of moral autonomy in Swiss democracy.

Looked at in this way what Habermas seems to "learn" from his look at "modernity" from the standpoint of the "challenge" of poststructuralism is the consequences of the rejection of the scheme of "subject-centered reason" for the philosophically critical intellectual, a scheme which gave shape to the utopian aspirations of the last century, and whose demise would lead to what Habermas calls "the new obscurity." Perhaps one might see his differences from his French antagonists in the way this "crisis" is thought about, diagnosed, and responded to. In conclusion I will select two issues that bring out this difference, from portions of the work of Foucault and of Derrida to which Habermas pays no attention.

Liberalism (Foucault)

There are two basic propositions of Habermas' own "discourse on modernity." There is the assurance that with "modernity" there is no further need for global progressive change in society; with "modernity" societies would have already reached their best, and therefore, final general shape, and the critical question becomes one which is internal to them. And there is the assurance that at bottom all the oppressions or problems we can legitimately contest in "modern" societies derive from the fact that we are prevented from freely discussing them. These two assurances support Habermas' solution to the dilemma of nineteenth-century utopian critique: a liberalism backed up by a transcendental theory of the act of human communication.

Habermas maintains that there must be a utopian side to any social critique. The crisis of "praxis philosophy" or the utopianism of human Labor, is therefore a crisis in the very possibility of social critique. He thinks it leads to a "new obscurity" of which the neostructuralists are the symptom. In this respect Habermas is the figure of the despair or exasperation of the social utopianism of the last century.

The sort of solution Habermas proposes for this dilemma runs throughout his work. He proposes to locate utopia not in labor, but in the supposed existence of quasi-transcendental presuppositions and aspirations of the act of communicative speech. Thus he proposes to reinterpret "alienated labor" as labor whose conditions are not open to a free or unconstrained discussion.

As Habermas' thought develops so does his conception of this communications utopia. At first he located it in such things as psychoanalytic therapy. But increasingly he came to locate it in a rational proceduralism that would underlie liberal democracy. It is those procedures, and those procedures alone, which he comes to think realize the utopian aspirations of human speech. In this way he confronts the traditional opposition between liberalism and social utopianism. He concludes that utopian thought must renounce any attempt to envisage an ideal way of life, and shrink to the acceptance of a formal proceduralism. He says: "The utopian content of the communications community shrinks to the formal aspect of an undamaged intersubjectivity. Even the expression 'ideal speech situation' leads to error in so far as it suggests a concrete way of life."[28] All our hope, all our political imagination, must reside solely in our capacity to formulate in advance the rational procedures of our discussion, and to use them to justify our democratic institutions.

Foucault had a different attitude to both social utopianism and liberalism, and a different conception of the relation of critical intelligence to them. He thought social utopianism was not good or bad in itself, and that it is misguided to think that all that is oppressive in our society is what prevents its realization. Utopia is one way people have used to envisage a form of political or social rationality. And, of course, there have been "administrative" utopias; Jeremy Bentham's *Panopticon* is one example.

The notion that intellectuals today might have other critical tasks from that of imagining a utopia did not strike him as either impossible or despairing. We should not believe that the source of the despair or hopelessness of people resides in the incapacity of intellectuals to offer them a utopian social vision, but in the actual material conditions of their existence, and the struggles or forms of power, in which they are caught. That is why it is important today for intellectuals to try to analyze as specifically and precisely as possible, the actual dangers they face.

It is this critical attitude that Foucault brought to his thinking about "liberalism," to which he devoted his course at the Collège de France in 1979. His idea was that

Liberalism is evidently not an ideology or an ideal. It is a very complex form of government and of governmental "rationality."

> It is, I believe, the obligation of the historian to study how it
> could function, at what price, and with what instruments—this,
> of course, for an epoch and in a given situation.[29]

Accordingly, Foucault had a different response to the perceived
"crisis," in the '80s, of the tax-and-transfer system that took shape
after the first War, with a view to minimizing social conflict, and
resolving the problems posed to parliamentary democracy by the
new sorts of labor associations.[30] It was more than a problem for a
workerish utopian imagination. It raised an analytic or conceptual
and a strategic problem about the "governmental rationality" or
the redistributive institutions: one could not see what else to do
except to manage or administer them in slightly different ways. In
looking at this impasse, Foucault thought we should avoid regard-
ing the welfare system as a cancerous growth, a source of premodern communitarian nostalgia, or a "Manichean" struggle between
the life-worlds and the administrative state. One should look at it
as a problem in how, at what price, and with what instruments a
form of historical rationality functions. In examining this history,
Foucault thought that the old liberal opposition between state and
civil society should be regarded as a "quasi-polemical" concept,
whose intelligibility depended on what it purported to analyze: the
event of a "bio-political" rationality in the way people govern
themselves and one another. That is the real danger we must confront.

Nationality (Derrida)

Derrida has long been interested in conceptions of nationality and
translation in philosophical traditions, and in the way they figure
in histories of philosophy. The history of philosophy Habermas
calls the "philosophical discourse of modernity" is hardly an exception: the question of German nationality was central to it. Indeed Lacoue-Labarthe thinks it provides a key to the questions: "1.
Why is German philosophy, since the first succession to Kant,
essentially philosophy of history? 2. Why is history, in such a philosophy, essentiality itself?"[31]

For the entire "discourse on modernity" was tied up with the
question of German aesthetic and philosophical identity, or the
lack of it. Indeed historians have often attributed the "anti-Enlight-
enment" features of this discourse to the German response to mo-

dernity. The question of German identity starts early on, and is found in Winckelmann's statement in 1775 "the only way for us to become great, or, if this is possible, inimitable, is to imitate the ancients," which supplies the title of one of Lacoue-Labarthe's books. It is also obviously central to the contributions the philosophical discourse of modernity made to national socialism, or to the part of it, which Lacoue-Labarthe calls "national aestheticism." [32]

Assertions of philosophical and cultural nationalism, of course, figure in Heidegger's views on the Germans as the "metaphysical people" and the German language as the primary philosophical language to take over from Greek and Latin. Such assertions form part of what Derrida thinks is urgent to question in Heidegger's thought for us today. But the same sorts of assertions are found as well in the work of all of Habermas' heroes or on the "rationalist" side of the dialectic of the Enlightenment; indeed as participants in the "discourse of modernity" Foucault and Derrida are the exception to the rule. Such assertions are found in Kant, in Hegel, and in Fichte, who said: "It is first of all the Germans who are called upon to begin a new era as pioneers and models for the rest of mankind." [33] The example of Fichte shows how philosophico-aesthetical German nationalism was thought quite compatible with Kant, and Enlightenment ideals.

The theme of German nationalism receives an ambiguous treatment in Habermas' book. On the one hand, it is not systematically linked to the "philosophical discourse of modernity." And yet in the authors he selects, and the line of descendence he traces, the "philosophical discourse of modernity" is the *German* philosophical discourse of modernity. On the other hand, just what Habermas thinks is specifically "German" (and thus later French) in this discourse is what he wants to eliminate from it: "What is perhaps specifically German is the philosophical concept of alienation both in the Hegelian Marxist version and then in the early Romantic version taken up by Nietzsche. The same theme resonates . . . in post-structuralist France." [34] Fichte thought the Germans were called upon to be pioneers for mankind. For Habermas they have become the models not of modernity, but of the errors of the Romantic rejection of it.

One is led to ask whether the *deus ex machina* of a procedural intersubjectivity helps to answer two questions about nationality and tradition: 1. How to conceive of "nationality" or "people"

outside the scheme that derives from Romanticism and its connections to "modernity" (This has a direct sense for contemporary
divided Germany).[35] 2. Whether other "peoples" confronted with
"modernization" or "Westernization" (as Germany did a century
ago) might find other ways of thinking about who they are as a
people than the ones that come from the nineteenth-century ideas
of nation, state, and society, which Hegel "elevated" to philosophy
in his discourse on modernity.

Questions of, or about, nationalism and liberalism, were, of course,
ones which preoccupied the nineteenth-century, when the very idea
of "the intellectual" was born. They are also ones which the events
of National Socialism and the War raised again in a particularly
acute manner, with which we are perhaps not yet fully done. In
raising such questions today, Habermas' book serves to shake things
up. But his own morality play of the battle between reason and
unreason may not offer the best way of thinking about them. Perhaps one might instead start with a remark Foucault made almost
a decade ago: "The failure of the major political theories nowadays
must lead not to a nonpolitical way of thinking but to an investigation of what has been our political way of thinking during this
century."[36]

NOTES

1. In an interview with Stephen Riggins in *Ethos* (Autumn 1984), pp. 1,
2, Foucault recalls his youth: "What strikes me now when I try to recall
those impressions is that nearly all the great emotional memories I have
are related to the political situation. I remember very well that I experi-
enced one of my first great frights when chancellor Dollfuss was assassi-
nated by the Nazis in, I think, 1934. It is something very far from us now. I
remember very well that I was really scared by that. I think it was my first
strong fright about death. I also remember refugees from Spain arriving in
Poitiers. I remember fighting in school with my classmates about the
Ethiopian War. I think boys and girls of this generation had their child-
hood formed by these great historical events. The menace of war was our
background, our framework of existence. Then the war arrived. Much
more than the activities of family life, it was these events concerning
the world which are the substance of our memory. I say our because I am
nearly sure that most boys and girls in France at this moment had the same
experience. Our private life was really threatened. Maybe that is the
reason why I am fascinated by history and the relationship between
personal experience and those events of which we are a part" (p. 5).

2. Habermas, *The Philosophical Discourse of Modernity* (Cambridge: MIT, 1987), p. 59.

3. *Ibid.*, pp. 183, 192.

4. "Posties," *London Review of Books*, Sept. 3, 1987, p. 11. It is amusing to note that Rorty was himself a much more fervent "postie" certainly than Foucault, but even than Derrida (see, for example, the discussion of a "post-philosophical culture" in *Consequences of Pragmatism*). Rorty's change of heart is apparently what he means by "keeping the conversation going." The latest candidate for unsolicited "solidarity" with Richard Rorty turns out to be Cornelius Castoriadis.

5. Habermas, *Philosophical Discourse*, p. 295.

6. See "The Dialectics of Rationalization" of 1981, reprinted in *Habermas, Autonomy and Solidarity*, Peter Dews, ed. (Verso, 1986), pp. 93–131. In the *Philosophical Discourse of Modernity*, Adorno and Horkheimer are credited with a more subtle superior view, one which one might not have noticed on first reading. ". . . under the sign of a Nietzsche revitalized by post-structuralism, moods and attitudes are spreading that are confusingly like those of Horkheimer and Adorno. I would like to forestall this confusion" (p. 106).

7. Foucault, *L'Impossible Prison* (Paris: Seuil, 1980), p. 317.

8. *Ibid.*, p. 318

9. Foucault, "La Vie et la science," in *Revue de Métaphysique et de Morale*, Janvier-Mars 1985, p. 5.

10. "What Is Enlightenment?" in *The Foucault Reader*, Paul Rabinow, ed. (New York: Pantheon, 1984), p. 46

11. Foucault, *L'Impossible Prison*, p. 46.

12. Foucault, *The Archeology of Knowledge* (New York: Harper, 1972), p. 9.

13. Habermas, *The Philosophical Discourse of Modernity*, p. 239.

14. Gary Gutting has studied in detail Foucault's relation to the history of science in Bachelard and Canguilhem; he establishes rather clearly that Foucault never held the caricatural anti-rationalist views Habermas attributes to him. *Michel Foucault and the History of Reason* (Cambridge: Cambridge University Press, forthcoming).

15. See Foucault's own remarks in *L'Impossible Prison*, p. 35: "When I speak of a 'disciplinary' society, one oughtn't understand a 'disciplined society.' When I speak of the spread of the methods of discipline, it is not to affirm that 'the French are obedient'! In the analysis of the procedures that are put into place to normalize, there is no thesis of a massive normalization. As if, precisely, all those developments were not measured by a perpetual lack of success"; and further (p. 37), where he says that the "automaticity" of power is not the thesis but the object of his study; and where he says that his analysis of discipline as not a "global analysis of society." In this and in other matters, Habermas may have been misled by the interpretation of Foucault offered by Dreyfus and Rabinow, who pre-

sent Foucault, in the style of Heidegger's views on technology, as having thought "that the increasing organization of everything is the central issue of our time." In *Michel Foucault: Beyond Structuralism and Hermeneutics*, (Chicago: University of Chicago Press, 1982), p. xxii. In a paper read at the symposium "Michel Foucault, philosophe" (Paris: Seuil 1989), Dominique Janicaud says that it would appear as if Habermas took Foucault as attempting to complete a "systematic philosophy," as though Habermas were more familiar with Dreyfus and Rabinow than with the actual work of Foucault ("Rationalité, Puissance et Pouvoir: Foucault sous les critiques de Habermas").

16. Foucault, "The Discourse on Language" in the *Archeology of Knowledge*, p. 234.

17. Derrida, *La Verité en peinture* (Paris: Flammarion, 1978), p. 25; English trans. (Chicago: University of Chicago Press, 1987).

18. Habermas, *The Philosophical Discourse of Modernity*, p. xix.

19. *Ibid.*, p. 16.

20. *Ibid.*, p. 37.

21. *Ibid.*, p. 65.

22. *Ibid.*, p. 45.

23. *Habermas and Modernity*, Richard Bernstein, ed. (Cambridge: MIT Press, 1985), p. 197.

24. Habermas, *The Philosophical Discourse of Modernity*, p. 16.

25. Marcel Detienne, *L'Invention de la mythologie* (Paris: Gallimard, 1981). For a more general discussion of the question by a philosopher influenced by Derrida, see Jean-Luc Nancy "Le mythe Interrompu" in *La Communauté désoeuvrée* (Paris: Bourgois, 1986), pp. 107–174 (English translation forthcoming from University of Minnesota Press).

26. Lacoue-Labarthe and Nancy, *L'Absolu Littéraire* (Paris: Seuil, 1978), English translation (Albany: SUNY Press, 1988).

27. There is a line which connects this discussion of "literary community" to *democracy*, a crucial theme for Habermas. (Rorty takes the theme of his book to be that democracy and neostructuralism are mutually exclusive). Among the philosophical conceptions on modern democracy are those which see its innovation as lying in the rejection of an essentialist or totalitarian conception of the social bond. Looking at the actual Declaration of the Rights of Man, and asking whether man has those rights in virtue of having an essential nature, Claude Lefort come to this conclusion: "What distinguishes democracy is that, if it inaugurated a history in which is abolished the place of the referent from which the law *(la loi)* gains its transcendence, it does not, by the same token, make the law immanent to the order of the world, nor, at the same time, confound its reign with that of power. It makes of the law what, always irreducible to human artifice, gives meaning to the action of men only on the condition that they wish it, that they apprehend it, as the reason of their coexistence and the condition of the possibility of each to judge and be judged. The division between the

legitimate and the illegitimate does not materialize itself in social space; it is only removed from certainty, when no one can occupy the place of the great judge, when this vacancy *(vide)* maintains the exigency of knowledge. In other words, for the notion of a regime regulated by laws, of a legitimate power, modern democracy invites us to substitute that of a regime based on *the legitimacy of a debate on the legitimate and the illegitimate*—a debate necessarily without guarantee and without end." *Essais sur le politique* (Paris: Seuil, 1986), p. 52. This is, of course, to say something different from the view that democracy is the political realization of the "unifying, consensus-building power of reason." One difference concerns the question of history, or "modernity," in the aesthetic or literary "genre" of discourse. How does this "democratic" conception of our relation to this law that nothing can embody concern the "community" of those involved with "literature"? In Derrida's paper "Prejugés," where the question of the "literary community" is raised, there is reference to a similar conception of the "unrepresentable structure of the law," or of judgment whose law is the absence of given criteria of judgment: "If these criteria were simply available, if the law was present, there, before us, there would be no judgment. ... there would be no place in it to judge or to worry about judgment; there would no longer be any place in it to ask how to judge." *La Faculté de juger* (Paris: Minuit, 1985), p. 94. Derrida links this "opening" in judgment to the question of literature. He advances, or at least entertains, the hypothesis that "the relatively modern specificity of literature as such [as distinct from 'poetry' or 'belles-lettres'] keeps an essential and tight relation with the history of law *(droit)*" (p. 32). "Literature" he suggests "has perhaps come, in historical conditions that are not simply linguistic, to occupy a place always open to a subversive judicity ... (where) self-identity is never reassuring" (p. 34). He asks whether the community of "critics, academics, theoreticians of literature, writers, philosophers" has not come to be formed in this space (of which he reads Kafka as offering a parable). This of course does not mean that those who are involved with literature must be democrats in political outlook. It is rather that the "question of literature" (as distinct from poetry or belles-lettres) involves the question of judgment before the "vacancy" of the law, which, for Lefort, would distinguish the "democratic revolution." This is what would require a different account of "community" or "solidarity" than that of the "unifying, consensus-building power of reason" in which the modern world would find an equivalent for God. For an account of *ancient* democracy, and its relations with myth and tragedy, in terms of the "relation to the law," see Nicole Loraux, *L'Invention d'Athènes* (Paris: Mouton, 1981); English translation (Cambridge: Harvard University Press).

28. Habermas, "The New Obscurity," in *Philosophy and Social Criticism.*

29. *L'Impossible Prison,*

30. See Foucault with Roberto Bono "Un système fini face à demande infinie," in *Sécurité Sociale: L'enjeu* (Paris: Syros, 1983); English translation, *History of the Present #2*, Spring 1986.

31. Lacoue-Labarthe, *L'Imitation des modernes* (Paris: Galilée, 1986), p. 88.

32. Lacoue-Labarthe, *La Fiction du politique* (Paris: Bourgois, 1987); English translation: forthcoming Basil Blackwell.

33. Johann Gottlieb Fichte, *Address to the German Nation*. In "Geschlecht II, The Hand of Heidegger," in *Deconstruction and Philosophy*, John Sallis, ed. (Chicago: University of Chicago Press, 1987), Derrida refers to a passage in the *Address to the German Nation* concerning the "race" *(Geschlecht)* of those who would educate, form, or reform mankind or humanity. It is an instance of a paradoxical link between nationalism and cosmopolitanism, which Derrida finds in many places. The characteristic doctrines of German "aesthetic-nationalism" were, of course, taken over by Carlyle and used to justify British Imperialism. Carlyle influenced Emerson's American nationalism, which recurs in Rorty's picture of nineteenth-century "pragmatic" America as the "hope of the nations."

34. *Habermas and Modernity*.

35. These lines were written before the events in East Germany of the end of 1989.

36. Foucault, *Technologies of the Self* (Amherst: University of Massachusetts Press, 1988), p. 161.

Part II

A STYLE OF PHILOSOPHY

THREE

Foucault The Philosopher: Ethics and Work

A PHILOSOPHER IN SPITE OF HIMSELF

I am not sure that Foucault always wanted to see himself as a philosopher. In an interview with some Marxist geographers in 1976, he declared ". . . Western Philosophy, since Descartes at least, has always been involved with the problem of knowledge. This is not something one can escape [. . .] And yet, however much I may say that I am not a philosopher, if it is nevertheless truth I am concerned with, then I am, in spite of everything, a philosopher."[1] Perhaps, in this concern for truth, Foucault would thus be a philosopher in spite of himself.

I think that this desire to say he was not a philosopher, to maintain a distance in relation to himself as a philosopher, formed part of his practice of thought. His relation to "the Tradition" was not a relation of identification, but had always to be sought; it was an open question, a question for the *practice* of thought. He did not conceive of his own work, nor that of his predecessors, as a homogeneous whole with eternal or completed boundaries; rather he

This lecture was given at a symposium, "Michel Foucault, Philosophe," January 1988, published by Editions du Seuil, Paris, 1989.

sought the ruptures, the cracks, the contingencies, and the re-elab-orations in what presents itself as the Tradition. "The problem of knowledge" has not always been raised in the same way; it has itself a history. Philosophical reflection consists not so much in giving a definitive response to this question as constantly deform-ing and reinventing it. As Blanchot says, Foucault was always a "man on the move."[2]

The diversity of the "we's" who are discussing him together today is a good indication of the diversity of his relations to philos-ophy.[3] We have different readings not only of Foucault, but also of philosophy. Michel Foucault the Philosopher is not a single thing. But perhaps this diversity itself comes from a two-pronged philo-sophical practice: on the one hand, a relation to what is given as "philosophical," and, on the other, to what is not, or not yet.

The first practice, or the relation to the already-philosophical would have as its principles: Do not suppose or construct a general history of Western Philosophy and try to find a place in it. Start instead from the idea that the tradition is not a single thing, and that the map of ways of thinking is always to be redrawn. Question the general schemes of its history, disperse them, open them to other questions. "For myself, I prefer to utilize the writers I like . . . to deform (their thought), to make it groan and protest."[4]

The second practice, or the relation to the non- (or the not-yet-) philosophical would ask us: Go *outside* philosophy, to use Deleuze's expression; put philosophy to the test of questions that seem for-eign or external to it. Make the art of thinking an art of delimiting new problems, around which would form new ensembles, which did not preexist them.

The first practice can be seen in Foucault's remarks on the begin-nings of contemporary philosophy in France in the '30s. Foucault distinguished a philosophy of formal relationality from a philoso-phy of subjective consciousness—the tradition of Cavaillès from the tradition of Sartre.[5] He was struck by the fact that Cavaillès, who gave his life to the Resistance, found *engagement* rather more simple than did any of the philosophers of *engagement*.

Those English-speaking philosophers accustomed to accepting Frege's criticism of Husserl's psychologism, and its radicalization through Wittgenstein's public practices of language, might find this dichotomy a rather familiar one. Starting in 1935, Cavaillès was interested in Wittgenstein, Frege, and Carnap, and, rejecting the philosophy of consciousness, he studied the foundations of mathematics and set theory. English-speaking philosophers might thus admire that Foucault took the side of Cavaillès against Sartre and sought a way out of phenomenology.

But conversely, these philosophers might be surprised to learn from the writings of Foucault of the '60s, that phenomenology and positivism, despite their well-known antagonisms, derive from common "archeological" grounds. They might be surprised by the "fork" described in *The Order of Things* in which the "being of language" leads, on the one hand, Russell, and, on the other, to Freud.[6]

Foucault proposed new readings of Freud and of Nietzsche. No one before him had situated the central event in the thought of Freud in his rupture with the theory of degeneracy. No one before him read Nietzsche in relation to Bachelard and Canguilhem, or in relation to the "new history" of the Annales School, or to the question of ideology in the struggles of the '60s, or even to the history of madness. And yet Foucault was not a "Nietzschean"; it was rather that he reread Nietzsche in terms of these new questions and not simply those of the thirties. In short, Foucault wanted to loosen the boundaries that had segmented philosophical intelligence, by introducing new questions into it, and taking up again those which history had bequeathed to us.

In accordance with the second practice, Foucault found these new questions in fields traditionally external to philosophy. He tried to show that the methods of the treatment of the mad belonged to the history of reason, and the art of constructing buildings to the history of ethics. "For me," he explained in 1975, "Nietzsche, Bataille, Blanchot, Klossowski, were ways out of philosophy," ways of making "permeable and therefore derisory the boundary between the philosophical and the non-philosophical."[7] But for him, "outside" philosophy was not simply this "literary" discourse; there was also the nineteenth-century medicine of deviancy and the eighteenth-century police science. He wanted to write at once for prisoners and philosophers. Even John Searle, who sought to transcribe the archeology of *énoncés* into a theory of speech-acts, recounts how Foucault taught him that masturbation might be the object of a philosophical interest.

Thus I would say that it is precisely in these attempts, these *essais*, to open philosophy outside itself that Foucault was a philosopher—a philosopher in spite of himself. What sort of "concern for truth" did this practice involve?

THE ETHOS OF PHILOSOPHY

I believe that in his Preface to the *Uses of Pleasure*, Foucault tried to thematize this attitude toward himself as a philosopher, and toward philosophical traditions, as that of an *ethos*, a way of being a philosopher. He held that philosophical discourse is always derisory when it claims to be a meta-discipline that fixes the legitimate borders, and supplies the unity of, all the other disciplines. What is "alive" in philosophy are rather the attempts to change it in relation to what seems foreign to it.

Thus the work of Foucault does not unfold as a theory or a system; it is punctuated by periodic attempts to rethink what was already thought in his work: "to think otherwise what one had already thought and to perceive what has been done from a different angle and in a clearer light."[8] The relation to oneself in one's work would thus be that of an exercise in which one becomes who one is while freeing oneself from oneself *(en se déprenant de soi)* .

Those whose ethos is that of this *déprise de soi* inhabit, he says, "another planet" from those who seek a fixed point of certainty or an authentic path or choice. And it is for this reason that in the history of philosophy he did not seek a tradition or a "we" with which to identify, but the specification of the singular events from which we never come back and which never leave us the same. It is this conception of a relation to oneself as a philosophical ethos, or way of being, that was at work in Foucault's attempt to rethink the traditions we call "ethical."

ETHICS IS NOT MORALITY

The traditions of ethical philosophy are not given to us as a unified whole. Even what we call Judeo-Christian morality was formed through a sort of collage of pagan sources. There have been changes not only in the codes which govern conduct, but also in the very conception of ethics—its central questions, what it supposes is true of ourselves, and the sorts of relations it is supposed to have with religion, science, politics, and law.

Foucault's idea was that what one had not sufficiently studied or thought about in the history of the origins and transformations of ethics, were the practices through which, in speaking truths about themselves, people were incited to form their ways of being. Accordingly, he set out to examine the history not of moralities or of moral codes, but of ethics, of "true" ways of being.

This distinction between morals and ways of being is one that runs throughout Foucault's work. In *The Order of Things*, Foucault doubted whether it was still possible for philosophy to underwrite moral codes in the manner of ancient cosmologies, with a theory of a Republic of civic or juridical subjects. "For modern thought, no morality is possible . . . thought . . . is in itself an action—a dangerous act."[9] This conception of "danger" would always be present in his ethic of thought.

The connection between thought and ways of being was already the focus of his study of the anthropological theme in Kant, and of what Kant had called "the pragmatic point of view." This connection was examined from another angle in Foucault's attempt to analyze penality from the standpoint of the new techniques for "governing" individuals which made of criminality an object of knowledge as well as a way of being. Foucault asked himself whether an actual exercise of power was not hidden under its traditional legal face. Instead of analyzing Sovereignty in terms of the subjects of a positive or natural right, he sought to analyze the historical and material constitution of subjects. Instead of conceiving of the individual in terms of his political status, he tried to pose to the conception of this status the question of the very "fabrication" of individuals.

Thus his way of conceiving the distinction between ethics and morality differed from the neo-Kantian opposition between *Moralität* and *Sittlichkeit*, on which was built a certain "philosophical discourse of modernity." For it was a question neither of inserting oneself in a beautiful totality, natural or essential, nor of raising oneself up to a transcendental republic, normative and rational. It was not a matter of deriving solidarity from rationality. Nor was it a matter of recovering a lost feeling of Community within Modern Reason. It was rather a matter of studying the practices of the self in terms of an intelligence that was proper to them, and from this standpoint, of posing the question of their place in a given society. It is in this respect that Foucault's "practices of the self" would be like Wittgenstein's "forms of ordinary life," in which what is given as subjective would derive from common, or public, transformable practices.

Foucault thus asked himself not how the practices of the self carry the decisions of a culture, but how it happens that a culture has given to them a particular position. It is because he wanted to reformulate in this way the question of the ethical being of an individual that, in *The Care of the Self*,[10] he objected to the confused or elastic idea of an "individualism" that would be invoked to explain, in different periods, very diverse phenomena. It is useful, he said, to distinguish the practices of the self which take the individual as an object of knowledge and action (as in Christian asceticism) both from the value given to the individual in the groups of which he is a member (as in a military aristocracy) and the value given to private or family life (as in the bourgeoisie of the nineteenth-century). Thus he wanted to distinguish the problem of individual freedom in ancient thought from "the platitude more or less derived from Hegel according to which the freedom of the individual would have no importance faced with the noble totality of the city."[11]

In studying ethics from the standpoint of the practices of the self, Foucault has outlined a history different from the ones found in Idealism or Romanticism. In this history, the formation of the individual would pass from Augustinian will to the "renaissance" of the idea of life as a work of art (as described by Burckhardt); it would pass from Descartes' cogito to Baudelaire's dandyism to Freud's confession. To distinguish ethics from morals in this way would then require that we reformulate the question of our own practices of the self in relation to modern politics and law.

THOUGHT AS AN ETHIC

If we allow, at least as a historical conjecture, this distinction between ethics and morals, can we apply it to the thought of Foucault itself? More precisely, can we conceive of his own practice of thought according to the four features he isolated in his study of ethics as a practice of the self?

1. The Substance. "The subject is not a substance. It is a form, and this form is not above all or always identical to itself . . . it is precisely the historical constitution of these different forms of the subject in relation to the play of truth that interests me."[12] What is to be transformed in this practice of the self is the self-evidence and the historical givenness of the forms through which the subject thinks he may truly identify himself. It is not the nature of the subject that is at issue but its "second nature"; not what is given, but what allows the subject the possibility of giving itself. The

substance is what, in the being of the subject, is open to a historical transformation.

2. The Mode of Subjection. It is the invitation to a practical freedom which incites this transformation: the chance of giving a "new impetus, as far and wide as possible, to the undefined work of freedom."[13] It is the possibility of making of freedom a practical and not simply a formal question—a freedom not of acts, intentions, or desires, but of the choice of a possible way of being.

3. The Ethical Work. The means of transformation would be those of a critical analysis that would reconstitute the forms of the subject as "transformable singularities."[14] We must determine precisely that against which we must struggle, to liberate ourselves and to liberate ourselves from ourselves. From the critical analysis of the "self-evidence on which rest our knowledge, our agreements, our practices"[15] is freed a "we" that is always "necessarily temporary."[16]

4. The Telos. The aims of this open transformation would be a practice of critically speaking of the truth, which no society can either regulate or silence; the beauty of risking oneself in a questioning of those events that are happening to us, in a "challenge to all phenomena of domination."[17]

Foucault's work, to the degree that all philosophical work implies an exercise of the self, and thus, in his sense, an ethic, might be resumed in the following way: in the name of a practical freedom, in what is given as possible forms of experience, to make a nominalist critical analysis that would give intelligence to the resistance to domination.

PROBLEMATIZATIONS

In his Preface to the *Uses of Pleasure*, Foucault wanted then to rethink what had already been done in his work according to a different light: the light of problematizations. There would exist a history of thought because there exists a history of the specific problems to which thought would have to respond. What, in the experience of criminality, of illness or madness, or of sexuality, would be given in such a problematic manner as to become something that had to be, and could be, thought?

His history of ethics was thus not a history of principles and their mode of legitimation, but of ways of thinking and responding to specific or singular problems. How had one conceived of the obstacles to overcome in order to be good, or to do one's duty? How had one rationalized what is to be done about what one thinks is evil or wrong? And, more precisely, how, from an analysis of problematizations, can we rethink the task of thought, in relation to knowledge, to strategies of action, to law, or to politics?

a. Knowledge-Power. According to what way of thinking had specific problems or dangers to oneself and to society become the objects of a possible knowledge and strategy? That was the question of his analysis of the system of thought whose great meta-concept is that of normality—a normality that would be absent from the problematization of Greek pleasures, but would be specific to our racism "in its modern, state, biologizing form."[18] How did the ancient practices of the self come to be colonized by this normalizing arrangement?

b. Law. How did new problems such as that of accident insurance become the object not simply of new legislation, but also a new way of conceiving of the law? One must analyze the law where its applications cause problems. One must study the history of the styles of legal reasoning that determine which sorts of object may fall under jurisdiction, by whom and how. This is the critical legal nominalism advanced by François Ewald: not a philosophy of the essence or nature of the law, but a history of the events or problematizations through which a singular "juridical experience" was constructed.[19]

c. Politics. In what way, under what conception, do problematic events become "political"? How do events become susceptible of a political settlement or debate? How do they come to transform the very concept of what is political—for example, that event whose name is a date: 1968? For Foucault, politics was not constitutive of problematizations; on the contrary, it was problematizations that posed questions to politics and obliged it to transform its conception of itself. It is in this sense that it is a question less of finding definitive solutions to problems as knowing how to introduce them into what is given as the political field.

This was the question that was raised by his analysis of the problematizations of the welfare-warfare state. How did a new problematization of life and death, a new way of governing ourselves, change not only the workings but also the very conception of the State? How did classical "liberal" thought, or the categories of State and Civil Society, emerge as a way of conceiving of this new biopolitics, and become problematized in turn? ". . . my way of approaching political questions . . . is on the order of problematizations, that is to say, the development of a domain of actions, practices, and thought, which seem to me to pose problems to politics."[20]

But the analysis of these dangers is itself also dangerous. For it is exercised in situations prior to normative-deductive reasoning, where one sees there exists something to be done without yet knowing what. A space is opened not of deduction but of analysis and questioning, in which one tries to determine the danger one does not yet see, but against which one must act. "The ethico-political choice" would consist in "determining which is the main danger." "I would like to do the genealogy of problems, or *problématiques*. My point is not that everything is bad, but that everything is dangerous, which is not exactly the same as bad. If everything is dangerous, then we always have something to do."[21]

POSSIBILITIES

The philosophy of Foucault is about what we can think and what we can change in what we think. The link between what is possible and what is thinkable goes back to Kant. Foucault wanted to introduce events into critical philosophy, and to advance a critical history of thought. For if our experience is made possible by categories, and if these categories themselves change, then it is equally our possibilities that change.

The task of critique becomes that of reconstituting the events in what is given as self-evidence—the events that make things conceivable. Thus, in the *Archeology of Knowledge*, Foucault talked of a historical a priori—an a priori not of legitimate boundaries, but of the historical possibilities of experience. But also for Foucault as for Kant, freedom was not one ethical possibility among others; it is the very possibility of ethics. "Ethics is the deliberate form assumed by freedom."[22] Contrary to Kant, this freedom is not supersensible, but historical. It does not derive from a rational Republic of autonomous agents, but from an incessant questioning of the historical givenness of our identity.

Foucault wanted to do a history not of what is true or false, but of what can be; not of what one must do, but of what can be done; not of how to live but of the possibilities of living. It is because he examined the historical possibility of knowledge, of action, and of subjective identity, that what he called knowledge was other than science, what he called power other than politics and what he called ethics other than morals. And the relations among knowledge, power, and ways of being are never given, but must always be sought; they are not essential or necessary, but historical and transformable.

In historicizing the critical question in this way, he discovered a kind of impossibility, which is not logical, but historical: the impossibility not of a round square or a nonexistent god, but the impossibility of what is no longer or not yet possible to think; not of what has no sense, but of what has it no longer or not yet. He raised the question of a historical constraint or exclusion, which it was the responsibility of the work of thought to bring to light.

This work on singular historical possibilities itself opened new philosophical possibilities, whose future remains fragile and uncertain; a new way of conceiving of the relations between philosophy and history, a new way of understanding the relation between philosophical *essais* and ways of being—in short, a new way of doing philosophy.

NOTES

1. Michel Foucault, *Power/Knowledge*, Colin Gordon, ed. (New York: Pantheon 1980), p. 66 (trans. modified).

2. Blanchot, *Foucault/Blanchot* (New York: Zone Books, 1987), p. 68

3. This paper was given at a symposium called "Michel Foucault, philosophe," in Paris, January, 1988, published at Seuil in 1989 under the same title.

4. Foucault, *Power/Knowledge*, p. 53–54.

5. Introduction to *The Normal and the Pathological* of Georges Canguilhem (New York: Zone Books, 1989).

6. Foucault, *Les Mots et les choses* (Paris: Gallimard, 1966), p. 312.

7. "Passe-frontières de la philosophie," *Le Monde*, September 6, 1986, trans. modified from *Michel Foucault, Politics, Philosophy, Culture*, Lawrence Kritzman, ed. (London: Routledge, 1988), pp. 312–313.

8. Foucault, *L'Usage des plaisirs* (Paris: Gallimard, 1985), p. 17.

9. Foucault, *Les Mots et les choses*, p. 339.

10. Foucault, *Le Souci de soi* (Paris: Gillimard, 1985), p. 56.

11. Foucault, "The Ethic of Care for the Self as a Practice of Freedom," in *Philosophy and Social Criticism* (Summer 1987), vol. 12. no. 2–3.

12. *Ibid.*

13. "What is Enlightenment?" in *Foucault Reader*, Paul Rabinow, ed. (New York: Pantheon, 1984), p. 46.

14. *The Foucault Reader*, p. 334.

15. *L'Impossible Prison*, Michelle Perrot, ed. (Paris: Seuil, 1980), p. 44.

16. *The Foucault Reader*, p. 385.

17. "The Ethic of Care for the Self as a Practice of Freedom."

18. *La Volonté de savoir* (Paris: Gallimard, 1976), p. 197.

19. François Ewald, *L'Etat Providence* (Paris: Grasset, 1986).

20. *The Foucault Reader*, p. 384.

21. *Ibid.*, p. 343.

22. "The Ethic of Care for the Self as a Practice of Freedom."

FOUR

Foucault's Art of Seeing

In his book called *Foucault*, Gilles Deleuze says of Michel Foucault that he was a great seer, a *voyant*. He declares that Foucault's seeing, and his discussion of seeing, are a constant and central part not only of his histories but also of his thought. He says that those who fail to take this part of his thought into account "mutilate" it to the point where it becomes comparable to analytic philosophy, something "with which it does not have much in common."[1]

Deleuze attributes many things to the visual part of Foucault's thought. The territory of the visual spans knowledge, art, ethics, and politics, and so it illustrates why Foucault had no difficulties in dealing with "the relations of science and literature, or the imaginary and the scientific, or the known and the lived."[2] The visual is also central to the way Foucault's thought would develop. It is the other component, along with "discourse," of what Deleuze sees as Foucault's "neo-Kantianism," and so it is linked to the theme of the "transcendental imagination" in Kant, and to the attempts on the part of Merleau-Ponty and Heidegger to go beyond intentionality to the "opening" of Being. But Deleuze also applies

This essay was published in *October* (Spring 1988), no. 4. It is reprinted here by permission of *October* and the MIT Press.

to Foucault the categories of the Danish semiologist Louis Hjelms-
lev that he had found useful in his study of film. He says that
Foucault was a great "audiovisual" thinker, who was "singularly
close to contemporary film."[3]

I think Deleuze is the first to "see" this side of Foucault's thought
and to demonstrate its general importance in his work.[4] I will not
follow all the intricate paths Deleuze gathers together in his analysis. I will try to present what I think Deleuze had in mind in
somewhat different terms. I start with Foucault's art of historical
depiction.

HISTORICAL PICTURES

Foucault was an exceedingly *visual* historian. His histories are
filled with vivid pictures that stick in the mind. Visualizing events
or historical depiction is, of course, an art which itself has a history. Events have not always been visualized in the same way or
under the same description. Michelet might be one example. So
would a whole aspect of the "new history" with which Foucault
associates his work in the Introduction to the *Archeology*, where an
attempt would be made to "turn documents into monuments"—
the preoccupation of the new historians with the "spaces" in which
people lived, and the reconstruction of *tableaux de moeurs*—the
sort of thing useful in making "period films."[5] But Foucault's pictures are more than such *tableaux*. They are puzzles that call for
analysis. They form part of a philosophical exercise in which seeing
has a part.

A frequent device in Foucault's writing is before-and-after pictures. One is shown a picture from one period and then one from
another. Thus the question of how one passed from one system of
thought to another is visualized. The device occurs throughout, but
is particularly prominent in the two "birth" books, the birth of the
prison and the birth of the clinic.

In *Discipline and Punish*, one is shown the picture of the excru-
ciating execution of Damiens, regicide, and then a timetable of
observed activities. In the *Birth of the Clinic* one is shown Pomme's
bathing cure of a hysteric in which the "heat" of her nervous
system is "dried out." And then one is shown Bayle's careful examination of the lesions in the brain, that "dingy-looking pulp."

In both cases we have pictures not simply of what things looked
like, but how things were *made* visible, how things were *given* to be

seen, how things were *"shown"* to knowledge or to power—two ways in which things became *seeable*. In the case of the prison, it is a question of two ways crime was made visible in the body, through "spectacle" or though "surveillance." In the case of the clinic, it is a question of two ways of organizing "the space in which bodies and eyes meet." With Bayle, the eye acquires depth, and the body, volume; in examining the brain he is looking into the depths of the individual body where disease is located. Pomme was still looking for that general "portrait" of the disease which allows for the classification of fevers.

In both instances Foucault links the two techniques of making things visible to a larger conception of seeing in the period. This is one theme in Deleuze—what he calls *visibilités*. There is a history not simply of what was seen, but of what could be seen, of what was *seeable*, or visible. A "visualization," a scheme through which things are given to be seen, belongs to the "positivity" of knowledge and power of a time and place.

But there is a second feature of Foucault's before-and-after pictures: the one which proposes a philosophical exercise in seeing. For, at the end of the analysis of the passage from before to after, one is led to "see" the depicted events in a new light, or in a different way—in the light of their underlying, unseen concepts. Thus, after reading *Discipline and Punish*, it is hard not to "see" annular prison construction in a new light, hard not to be surprised that "prisons resemble factories, schools, barracks, hospitals, which all resemble prisons."[6] This is the aspect of Foucault's historical depiction Deleuze calls *évidences*. Foucault would be a "seer" because of the way "visibility" and "evidence" are linked in his history, and in his thought.

VISIBILITY

Foucault finds in what he calls "the classical age" a whole range of ways of seeing, and of letting things be seen, which would have been unthinkable in the preceding period in which the eye was linked to the ear in the deciphering of "resemblances": in the classificatory tables of its forms of knowledge; in the primacy it accords to perceptual evidence; in its conception of madness as "dazzled reason"; in its conception of painting; in its utopian literature of the transparent society; in its natural histories as well as in its way of "displaying" mad people, so different from the "ship of fools." Foucault tried to determine the deep conceptual organization which gathered these seeings together into a form of "visibility" different from others.

Foucault's hypothesis was that there exists a sort of "positive unconscious" of vision which determines not what is seen, but what *can* be seen. His idea is that not all ways of visualizing or rendering visible are possible at once. A period only lets some things be seen and not others. It "illuminates" some things and so casts others in the shade. There is much more regularity, much more *constraint*, in what we can see than we suppose. To see is always to think, since what is seeable is part of what "structures thought in advance." And conversely to think is always to see.

What makes the visual intelligible is itself unseen. It is an anonymous body of practice spread out in different places. As Deleuze puts it, *"visibilités* are neither the acts of a seeing subject nor the givens of a visual sense."[7] In the *Archeology of Knowledge* Foucault discusses "enunciative modalities" as properties of discourse. But in his histories he also discusses "modalities of seeing" as properties of visual intelligence: who sees what or whom and where are integral features of the visual thinking of a period and not an independent fact about its contexts. And this visual thought is rooted in a specific sort of "material existence"—the spaces in which it is exercised (such as hospital, prison, museum, or home), and the techniques through which its images are reproduced and circulated (such as printing, markets, and so forth).

In one sense, it is "the subject" which is given in the forms of "visibility." Foucault finds that the same organization a period assigns to inner or psychological processes recurs in external "public" ones such as making maps or illustrating scholarly works. Thus the scheme of Renaissance resemblances is placed, by the classical period, within the imagination as a source of error to be cleared up by proper observation. And, with the birth of the clinic, the "visionary space" in which disease had been discussed is put into the head of the patient. Visualization belongs to the great internalizing or psychologizing practices Foucault associates with modernity. Thus, Freud's idea of dreaming as a way of showing to oneself one's innermost desires, contrasts with Artemidorus' scheme where dreams are ways of making visible one's fortune in a hierarchical society.[8]

The visual thinking of a period would thus have a positive organization. But that organization is not rooted in keeping something concealed. As Foucault came to realize, the "classical" way of making madness visible was not based on the repression or concealment of the true way of seeing it. The conceptual scheme that determines what can be seen is, in the phrase of the *Archeology*, "invisible but not hidden." The visibility of a period may be invisible to it, but not as something hidden or kept from sight. What is invisible is just the light which illuminates things or makes them visible.

In short, visibility is a matter of a positive, material, anonymous body of practice. Its existence shows that we are much less free in what we see than we think, for we do not see the constraints of thought in what we can see. But it also shows that we are much *more* free than we think, since the element of visibility is also something that opens seeing to historical change or transformation.[9] That is the problem of *évidence*.

EVIDENCE

Evidence, in both English and French, comes from *videre*, to see. In the course of its history, the word acquires the senses of proof, testimony, and clarity or indubitability to the mind. Ian Hacking has studied one change in the concept of evidence in his history of the "emergence of probability."[10] It is the one that made Hume possible.

There is one sense of the French word *évidence* which is particularly marked in Foucault's visual idiom—the one English translates as "self-evidence": what is taken for granted or accepted without question. Foucault introduces this concept of evidence into his historical depiction in a new way.

In a discussion with historians, Foucault explains that his way of seeing the birth of the prison was an attempt to see "events" behind self-evident entities and continuities, and so to "event-alize" history. One starts with a *rupture d'évidence*, a break with self-evidence, with "those *évidences* on which our knowledges, our agreements, our practices, rest."[11] And then one asks how such *"évidences"* arose and took form. Where there is self-evidence, one tries to uncover the singular formation of an event unseen.

Evidence is used in this sense in both birth books. Thus, in the *Birth of the Clinic*, Foucault says that "the exact superposition of the 'body' of disease and the body of the sick man . . . is *self-evident* only for us."[12] And, in *Discipline and Punish* he refers to the "self-evident character *(le caractère d'évidence)* that the prison form soon assumed."[13] There is both a legal and an economic self-evidence to the prison form; together they explain why, despite the fact that the prison was not doing what it was meant to do, "one could not 'see' how to replace it."[14]

"Seeing" in this sense is part of doing. We cannot see what to do because we are "prisoners" of the self-evidence of one *way* of seeing what to do. We participate, we do our bit, in the practices which make that way of seeing self-evident to us—a participation or acceptance we can refuse. Thus in Foucault's idiom, *évidence* is related to the *acceptability* of a practice. It is part of what makes a "strategy of power" *tolerable*, despite its difficulties. Thus, to see the events through which things become self-evident is to be able to see in what ways they may be *intolerable* or *unacceptable*. It is to try to see how we might *act* on what cannot yet be seen in what we do. It is, in short, a "critical" art, and it is in exercising it that Foucault would be, in Deleuze's term, a seer or *voyant*.

For Deleuze, a seer is not basically, nor in the first instance, someone who can depict future events. Nor is he necessarily the sort of "visionary" or "utopian" who looks forward to the place where everything that ought to be is finally made transparent to all.[15] "A seer," says Deleuze, "is someone who sees something not seen."[16] Foucault's art of seeing is an art of exposing the unseen *évidences* that make the things we in fact do acceptable or tolerable to us.

Deleuze finds this sort of seeing in the work Foucault did for the Group for Information about Prisons, of which Deleuze was a member. A kind of "public space" of discussion with prisoners was opened up. It was in this space that Foucault "saw something which at the time no one else saw." This act of seeing required a *rupture d'évidence:* the gap between the self-evidence of the economical and legal conception of the prison, and what was actually going on. In this gap one could start to see something intolerable in those practices, which opened up a question for historical analysis: an analysis that would initiate new ways of seeing and thinking not simply about French penal institutions, but also about the strategic organization of power in modern societies, its relations to forms of knowledge and modes of living. Foucault's seeing would lie in this critical opening in thinking. Says Deleuze:

He saw things, and like all people who know how to see something and see it deeply, he found what he saw to be intolerable. For him to think meant to react to the intolerable, to something intolerable that he had seen. And the intolerable was never the visible, it was something more.[17]

One sense of "evidence" in the study of history is the sense of the "eye-witness" to actual events as distinct from the "eye" that reads forthcoming events. Foucault's idea of the events of evidence has to do with the eye of *historians*. In *fictional* depiction, Foucault found a similar aim of making visible the unseen spaces of seeing. In Maurice Blanchot's depiction of the "space" in which encounters transpire and words are exchanged, he saw, in fiction, an attempt "not to show *(faire voir)* the invisible, but to show the extent to which the invisibility of the visible is invisible. Hence [fiction] bears a profound kinship with space."[18]

In several interviews, Foucault also describes his *own* histories as fiction. It is not that these histories lack the validity that would distinguish them from fiction. It is rather that they share an *aim* with fiction: the aim not of explanation, or of showing how our ways of seeing and doing are historically necessitated, but, on the contrary, of showing how things might be otherwise, beyond our self-evidences. That is why the history of the "evidences" of the way things are seen includes the "evidences" in the thinking of historians. To "see" is to open history to new domains and new questions, "to do this history of the 'objectification' of those events historians take as objectively given."[19] When Foucault says that he writes works of history that are more than works of a historian,[20] it is in part because of this other aim of seeing, which the philosopher would share with the writer.

Seeing is important in Foucault's work as philosopher and historian in this sense as an art of trying to see what is unthought in our seeing, and to open as yet unseen ways of seeing. A peculiar idiom of space and sight unfolds in Foucault's writing that moves in many directions. I would now like to bring various facets of this idiom into focus, to look at seeing in knowing, seeing in doing, seeing in thinking, and in living.

SEEING IN KNOWING

Foucault did not see knowledge as simply built up from ordinary perceptual evidence through a logic of inference, inductive or deductive. He was concerned with the ways seeing in knowledge has been itself conceptually constructed. In his idiom a *savoir* requires, and sets up, a way of *spatializing* itself, a sort of "technology of the visible." Foucault wanted to get away from what might be called our modern philosophical obsession with what we call "observation" in knowledge—a piece of philosophical "self-evidence" he found in different forms in both phenomenology and positivism. Our philosophical conception of observation is a recent one, and it prevents us from seeing how knowledge is *in fact* "spatialized" or "visualized." In science, seeing is more than meets the eye.

"Ocular metaphors," it has often been observed, occupy a central place in our vocabulary of knowing: truth is something we say we see. But these metaphors have not always worked in the same way. Foucault thought the changes were in part due to the *actual* ways people invented to "spatialize" their knowledge, the *actual* role of seeing in knowledge. Richard Rorty reviews the analytic literature which shows how the Cartesian idea of perception differs from the "hylomorphic" seeing in Scholastic thought; nature is mirrored in a new way.[21] But in Foucault's archeology of the visual, the emergence of the Cartesian privilege of perception, with its idea of evidence as transparency to the mind, is a rather more complicated one.

In the "Discourse on Language," there is talk of a general change in seeing that would arise in Britain of the sixteenth and seventeenth centuries, captured in the precept "look rather than read, verify rather than comment." It involved a whole "scheme of possible, observable, measurable, classifiable objects,"[22] a scheme which preceded the actual collection of the "contents" of knowledge. This change matches with what, in the *Order of Things*, Foucault calls a "reorganization of culture in which we are still caught," where the eye no longer deciphers the "prose of the world," and where, therefore, "the eye was . . . destined to see and only see, and the ear to hear and only hear."[23] There thus arises the doctrine of separation of the senses central to the emergence of the new discipline of "aesthetics" in Lessing and Diderot.[24]

In knowledge, one place we see the change is in the "spatialization" of the natural histories of the classical period. In the classifications of Linnaeus, plants were studied, without microscopes, in terms of their visual "character," the colorless, odorless, "primary qualities" of a planar space. The principle of classification of elements and their arrangement in this space was based on a sort of "optics" of plant morphology, one which could be shown through the illustrations the new printing techniques made possible, and one which figured in the account of the "reproduction" of the plants themselves. It is this conceptual reorganization or "spatialization" which made natural history "nothing more than the nomination of the visible." The "natural histories of the classical period," Foucault argues, "did not become possible when men looked harder and more closely,"[25] but when what they saw was organized in this new way.

The *Birth of the Clinic* records another change in seeing that occurs in French medicine at the end of the eighteenth century. Foucault is again at pains to dispute the view that "men looked harder and more closely." He disputes the account of the change in medicine in which the eye would move from fantastic imaginings to the careful observations of things. This is part of his general quarrel with the dichotomy between the imaginary and the epistemic, or the ideological and the scientific, in the history of knowledge.[26]

In fact, he argues, the "visionary space" in which doctors, physiologists, and patients discussed disease was itself a quite regular and coherent form of "spatialization," one based on recognizing the "portrait" of the disease in the body. And, what was involved in the "birth of the clinic" was a change in the whole idea of what it is to be "seen" by a doctor—where, with what instruments, and under what concepts.

Foucault argues that the change cannot be explained by "thematic contents," or "logical modalities," or the use of quantitative methods alone. It is the "space" of disease itself which changes, the place in the individual body where it is located, and the institutional "space" in which such localization occurs. Moreover, there was nothing inevitable about the change; one had to wait decades to get cures. The explanation for the change turns on institutional factors which emerge through the new programs of the French Revolution.

In this way, Foucault tries to show that it was the complex "spatialization" of disease which accounted for the role of observation in the new medicine, and not the primacy of observation which accounted for its new conception of illness. Such processes of "spatialization," however, are not the same thing as "theory-dependence." Foucault is not saying that medicine started to use a new theoretical vocabulary with which its "observation-reports" were "laden." It is rather a matter of the construction of a "space" in which not just observation, but also theory, becomes possible.

Foucault might be said in this regard to extend the distinction Georges Canguilhem had developed in his study of the reflex between "the history of theories" and the "history of concepts."[27] There is a history of the *concepts* through which things were given to be seen, which is separate from the history of *theories* about them. In particular, Foucault was interested in the history of how the concepts of visualization came to be embedded in institutional practices, or what he calls "tertiary spatialization." Thus, in *Discipline and Punish*, he goes on to explain that "One of the essential conditions for the epistemological 'thaw' of medicine at the end of the eighteenth century was the organization of the hospital as an 'examining apparatus.' " For through this "apparatus" was "established over individuals the visibility by which they were differentiated and judged."[28]

The spatial "scheme" of a form of knowledge is not only distinct from the theories which occur within it; it often precedes and makes them possible. Thus the singular manner in which the general hospital gave mad people to be seen precedes the elaboration of the classical theory of madness, and the architectural reorganization of prisons precedes the new theory of crime. The relation between theory and visualization in knowledge is not fixed or given as in the Kantian idea of a "schematism" locked in the recesses of the human soul. It is rather a matter of contingent historical configuration.

In asking how such entities as "madness," "illness," or "crime" were made visible in the knowledge of different periods, Foucault thus focused on practices of "spatialization" that were more complex, and more deeply embedded in external processes, than the mere exercise of the naked eye aided with a theoretical vocabulary. In his archeology of seeing in knowing, what he "excavated" was how the eye of observation was oriented in such practices, in a manner that does not simply derive from theory.

He thus revived an old philosophical debate about seeing and *reality*. From the fact that disease is "spatialized," does it follow that it is not "real"? Does it follow that when a physician sees a patient he is not seeing something real, but only the phantom of the discourse of his time? One source of such questions is the old idea that the real is what is observable.

Ian Hacking takes on just this idea in his discussion of the question, in the philosophy of the natural sciences, as to whether or not abstract or theoretical entities are real.[29] Hacking argues that it is the obsession with "observation" in the philosophy of the natural sciences that has obscured the recognition of the role of complex experimental apparatuses in what one might call the "visualization" of theoretical entities in physics or genetics. Natural science also has its "modes of spatialization"; there is a whole natural "technology of the visual" as there is a human one: observatories, microscopes, cyclotrons. And experimentation is central to them.

For Hacking, "observation" is a misleading inheritance of logical positivism. In apparent allusion to Foucault, he says that phenomenology and positivism both descend from a "change in seeing" that occurs around 1800. Then would be forged the link between what is observable and what is real. Thus, in Hacking's example, both phenomenologists and positivists can agree that while meatballs are real, mesons are not.

In particular Hacking says that the positivist preoccupation with observation has led to two philosophical themes which have conjointly obscured the role of experimentation in natural science: Willard Quine's idea of semantic assent, and Norman Hanson's idea of theory-laden observation. Together they have led to the obtuse idea that, in physical science, seeing is saying. In fact, verbal "observations reports" that test theories are quite rare in physics. What matters is rather that engineering that evokes or constructs entities in highly artificial conditions. The relation between experimental engineering and theory is a complex and variable one. It is a matter of history; it is not given in a "logic" of inferring theory from perception. To understand experiment is to understand the question of what makes modern science modern; for the link between theory and experiment is part of a larger history of the link between technology and science, which helped to determine the very sense we give to "technology."

Hacking writes in praise of Francis Bacon, philosopher of experiment. Bacon's idea not of observation, but of "prerogative instances" gives a better picture than Carnap's of the way theoretical entities are made visible. Thus Hacking proposes to substitute an experimental for an observational realism. As far as he is concerned, if you can spray electrons, then they are real—just as real as meatballs. He thinks that it is the Hanson-Quine idea that seeing is saying that has induced philosophical doubts as to whether or not there exist real entities outside the verbalizations of science. Experimentation is a corrective; it offers a better way of understanding the sense in which theoretical entities can be said to be real.

Foucault's archeology of the "spatializations" of madness or illness, while it disputes simple observational realism, nevertheless does not lead, in a parallel way, to the sort of "pragmatic realism" which says: if you can cure a patient, then the illness you have seen in him is real. On the contrary, it leads in the opposite direction of a sort of nominalism; and in the *Archeology of Knowledge*, for example, Foucault talks of "de-presentifying" the very things of which he writes the "archeology."[30]

Our knowledge is, of course, such that we can "do" things to illness or madness just as we can to electrons or genes. But seeing and doing are not related in the same way. In the case of illness or madness, the construction of seeing, and the way it fits in institutions and comes to be related to other fields, never loses contact with the way certain "real" social problems are seen.

There is one sense in which Foucault's question about how we "see" psychotics is a different *sort* of question from that of what we should do about atoms or genes—even if our best *theory* about psychosis should turn out to be a genetic one. For he is not asking what to do with the psychoses our knowledge lets us see, but whether we can or want to refuse the "evidences" of the way they are given to be seen in a whole range of practices, and invent other ways of seeing/dealing with them. It is this sort of interconnection between seeing, doing, and practical self-evidence to which he turns in *Discipline and Punish*. In that book he draws a distinction between disciplinary and Baconian ways of seeing.

A central topic is "normalization." "Normality" as a fundamental category of our behavior, and even of our identity, becomes "visible" through an expanding network of practices in the nineteenth century. One of the basic things our knowledge makes visible to us is *abnormalities* both of persons and of societies.

One source is precisely medicine, the change in what it means to be "seen" by a doctor. There has been no independent way of identifying illness except as the deprivation of the state of health in the whole body. Then physiological anatomy introduced criteria for being a diseased organ independent of the health of the whole person. "Normality" could be defined as the absence of pathological symptoms in the organs. Abnormality started to be related to degeneracy. All this was part of the change in the medical gaze:

when a doctor "saw" a patient he began to ask not "what is the matter with you?" but "where does it hurt?"

But this new rationality of the normal came to be applied in other places—for example, in Durkheim's attempt to distinguish "normal" from "pathological" states of societies, or to specify the "degenerate" portion of a population. The art of seeing "abnormality" fit within a network of practice. And it is the organization of that network that was rather different from the one that allows us to spray electrons.

In *Discipline and Punish*, the term "technology" enters Foucault's methodological lexicon. Discipline involves a new "technology of the visual." There is a comparison with experimental devices, and with Bacon, philosopher of experiment. As telescopes, microscopes, and prisms helped transform not simply what physics could see, but the place of "seeing" in it, so the techniques of surveillance and examination (that "microscope of behavior") not simply made such things as the "abnormal" or "criminal" personality visible; they also helped change the place of the visual in knowledge and power. These "observatories of human multiplicities," writes Foucault, introduced "an obscure art of light and the visible" which was "secretly preparing a whole new knowledge of man."[31]

And yet there is a basic difference between the two types of visual technology, or of the place of the visual "technique" in knowledge and power. "Another knowledge, another power," says Foucault. Then he refers to Bacon: "On the threshold of the classical age, Bacon, lawyer and statesman, tried to develop a methodology for the empirical sciences. What Great Observer will produce the methodology of examination in the human sciences?" But he quickly adds:

> Unless, of course, such a thing is not possible. For, although it is true that, in becoming a technique for the empirical sciences, the investigation has detached itself from the inquisitorial procedure, in which it was historically rooted, the examination has remained close to the disciplinary power that shaped it. It has always been and still is an intrinsic element of the disciplines.[32]

Bacon's conception of experiment may have roots in Inquisitorial procedure—putting Nature to the rack to extract her secrets—but the technique has long been cut loose from the sorts of problems the Inquisition was designed to deal with. In the case of discipline and its technology of seeing, its "art of light and the visible," by contrast, we see a process through which it multiplied and complexified its links to the problems it was designed to deal with; it spread out in a range of institutions where it retains the rationality of a "technical matrix."

In the difficulties that arose from the implementation of "hard" technologies such as the steam engine, the electric plant, or the television, the focus of the "problematization" was not on the "evidence" of seeing steam, electricity, or electrons. By contrast just what Foucault found important in anti-psychiatric protest or prison revolts was the way it questioned the very "technical matrix" of the disciplines which made the madman or the criminal visible; the way it exposed the very "evidence" through which those practices are accepted.

Thus the "philosophical" problem of "seeing electrons" is not at issue in the great questions of what to *do* with them, make war or energy. But the problem of "seeing psychoses" *is* involved in the questioning of what we should do about *them*. Seeing and doing are related in different ways. Another knowledge, another power. That is why the philosophical attitude toward one can be realistic, and toward the other, nominalistic. The realist of experiments and the nominalist of disciplines can agree that seeing in knowledge is a more complex matter than inferring from perception. For their differences lie in the way knowledge comes to be "visualized" or "spatialized."

SPACES OF CONSTRUCTED VISIBILITY

"Space" is a constant topic in Foucault's histories and in his thinking. As already indicated, it plays a prominent role in his study of medicine, and then it is taken up in a different way and generalized in his study of penal practices. The "spaces" we call the "territories" of states also become central in his study of the "police science" which helped introduce a new administrative sort of rationality, and a "geo-political" orientation and organization of war and diplomacy.

In the historical study of space, Foucault was impressed by the work of such social historians as Bloch, Braudel, and Ariès. He thought their work might serve as a corrective to one tendency in the philosophy of time in Bergson, Heidegger, and Sartre—the tendency of putting "space" on the side of the "pratico-inert," while reserving for time the great questions of project and history.[33]

A significant portion of Foucault's discussion of "space" is devoted to the problem of *visibility*—how spaces were designed to make things seeable, and seeable in a specific way. In his histories of the visual unthought, the construction of space plays a key role.

During the course of an interview devoted to space, Foucault declares:

> I think it is somewhat arbitrary to try to dissociate the effective practice of freedom by people, the practice of social relations, and the spatial distributions in which they find themselves. If they are separated, they become impossible to understand. Each can only be understood through the other.[34]

"The spatial distributions in which (people) find themselves"— that names a recurrent topos in Foucault's work: hospitals, poorhouses, museums, public baths, schools, homes, asylums are all spaces in which one can reconstitute the rationality of an elaborate construction of what can be seen. They are spaces of constructed visibility.

We are surrounded by spaces which help form the evidences of the ways we see ourselves and one another. Where we "dwell," how we are housed, helps in this way to determine who and what we think we are—and so they involve our freedom. We are beings who are "spatialized" in various ways; there is a historical spatialization of ourselves as subjects.

Foucault's analysis of "spaces of constructed visibility" brings out how they serve to "constitute the subject," the way they serve to construct the spatialization of the subject or his "being in space." "The art of light and the visible," which such spaces are designed to deploy, is one which makes certain *kinds* of properties of ourselves stand out as self-evident.

Foucault suggests it is just this link between visibility and constructed space that would make a "technological" history of the art of architecture possible. For the art of building is, among other things, an art of rendering visible, and so discovers one of its central interconnections with power. Architecture helps "visualize" power in other ways than simply manifesting it. It is not simply a matter of what a building shows "symbolically" or "semiotically," but also of what it makes visible about us and within us. Châteaux and churches may do this through the way they manifest divinity, sovereignty, and might. Before the museum, they may supply, as Malraux stressed, the central "imaginary" spaces which secure the categories through which art was given to be seen. But in Ledoux's salt mine Foucault finds another relation between power, visibility, and constructed space, one connected to new problems of poverty and work, one to which Bentham would give the name "panopticism." The construction of buildings is involved in the new "art of light and the visible," which doesn't look up to the glory of those who possess or embody power, but looks down to the marginalized anonymous mass that escapes it.

The art or technique of the visual in "panoptic" architecture is not exhausted by the wondrous contrivances that make the constant surveillance of the inmates of its enclosed space invisible to them. Panoptic establishments also inscribe in cellular stone the new sorts of classifications designed to deal with wayward populations. They are constructed to facilitate the introduction of the "examination" procedures that rank and judge people according to their "visible" characteristics. This spatialization makes the new classifications, unlike contemporary botanical ones, "disciplinary" —what makes a person classifiable submits him to an "individualizing" control. Thus Foucault says, where natural taxonomy links category and character, disciplinary tactics link the singular and the multiple; they give attention to each and every member of a multiplicity individually. They make the categories into which the "character" of people are slotted "visible" in them; they create in people an "individuality" that is endowed with certain "essential" or evident sorts of properties. Thus it is not simply that the "eye of power" looks down rather than up. What it sees is no longer heroic acts, but dysfunctional personalities. It focuses light not on illegal acts, but on behavioral deficiencies. It "spatializes" this new thing which is the "personality" of an individual.

Bentham's panoptic scheme is related to the "self-evidence" of his great moral principle of the rational calculability of the good of individuals. For one's good to be tabulated one must be "seen" in a certain way, or under certain categories, just the sort of categories architecture would serve to make visible. An art of spatializing human multiplicities would then be central to the formulation of utilitarian ethics.

Ludwig Wittgenstein tried to show that "looking within" or "introspection" was nothing more than a rule-governed art of language. Foucault's analysis of the rules that govern the art of space shows that when we look within we often see not so much our Cartesian minds as the worrisome sources of our behavioral deficiencies, but that in this, we are no less participating in a practice which makes the sort of thing we see seem self-evident to us.

SEEING IN POWER

"Spatialization" is thus one technique in the exercise of power. That is why it cannot be separated from the "effective practice" of our freedom, or our relations with one another. There is a political history of the visual unthought: a history of the way forms of power "visualize" themselves. A principle of this history is that "visibility" is one of the great "self-evidences" of the workings of power. Power becomes acceptable or tolerable through its spatialization or the way it is given to be seen.

Thus, in the *History of Sexuality*, Foucault says, "Power is *tolerable* only on the condition that it mask a substantial part of itself . . . would it be *accepted* if it were entirely cynical?"[35] One way it masks itself to get people to "see" it in a certain way. Power conceals itself by visualizing itself. Its workings become acceptable because one sees of it only what it lets one see, only what it makes visible.

We are fascinated by the pomp, the "ostentatious signs" of power. That contributes to the "self-evidence" of our idea that it is owned or possessed, where in fact it is being anonymously exercised. One reason we don't see discipline as the form of power that it is is that we don't see how it makes us visible. The inspector in the tower doesn't possess or embody, doesn't *see*, the power he implements. The sort of "visibility" the disciplines introduce conceals not simply how they work, but what they are. We don't "see" discipline as power, because we don't "see" power as strategy.

In particular the techniques for visualizing power as sovereignty, nobility, and law have prevented us from seeing it as anonymous technique. In the *History of Sexuality*, Foucault suggests how this proposition might be applied to the analysis of fascism. Something as the neo-Classical facades of panoptic prison architecture concealed the strategic construction of visibility within, so the great fascist "premodern" rituals of the ostentation of sovereignty, law, and blood concealed the very "modern" way its power in fact was working, and so helped to make it tolerable.

SEEING THROUGH DESIRE

In the *History of Sexuality*, Foucault introduces another theme: the history of the sort of *pleasure* we take in what we see. He came to think that it is because it belongs to what we conceive of as our "sexuality" that we are *fascinated* by it, that we want to *expose* (or *exhibit*) it, a fascination and an exposition which are linked to *knowing* it, or to the sort of truth it might tell us about ourselves: "We have invented" declared Foucault, "a peculiar pleasure in knowing that truth, in discovering it and exposing (or exhibiting) it, the fascination of seeing it and telling it."[36] It has not always been this way. What has been taken to be most glorious or problematic about our sexual experience has not always been this thing that fascinates us, and which we must expose; the "spaces" and "techniques" which give it to be seen in this way have not always been with us. We have not always been fascinated by our sexual *desire*, this dangerous thing Freud would be the first to have the courage to look at straight on.

Foucault wanted to determine how the "self-evidence" of this sexuality we must show and see arose in our knowledge, our agreements, and our practices. One place he looked was in what might be called the "voyeurism" of the nineteenth-century medicine of sexual deviancy: its special curiosity, its prurient preoccupation with its object—a "fascination" structurally not so unlike the "pornographic" search of one's "secret life." Foucault takes this interest as a historical property of a medical discourse and practice, not as a quirk of the doctors taken individually. But it was also a property of the "spaces" they worked in, a fact about a medical art of making sexuality visible, an incitement to see and show its dangerous truth.

One example is Jean-Marie Charcot's La Salpêtrière, where Freud made his "discovery" of the unconscious. That space was not simply a space of constructed visibility, but also a space of the *incitement* to see. "It was an enormous apparatus for observation, with its examinations, interrogations and experiments." But it was also:

> a machinery for incitement, with its public presentations, its theatre of ritual crises, carefully staged with the help of amil nitrate, its interplay of dialogues, palpitations, laying on of hands, postures which doctors elicited or obliterated with a gesture or a word, its hierarchy of personnel who kept watch, organized, pro-

voked, monitored, and reported, and who accumulated an immense pyramid of observations and dossiers.[37]

And yet it refused to *name* what it thus incited to see: sexuality.

Charcot was said to be, and called himself, *un grand visuel*. And in his obituary, Freud says of Charcot that he was an artistically gifted seer, that the chaos of symptoms was set in order by the eye of his spirit, that he talked incessantly about the merits and difficulties of seeing in the ward of the sick, in which he said he found his greatest *satisfaction*. But, adds Freud, while he was a seer, a *visuel*, he was not a thinker or a "brooder." He could not *name* theoretically what he saw. In this obituary we see the beginnings of what, for Freud, it would mean to "observe" the processes of unconscious desire.

Charcot invented a differential diagnostic scheme for the various "types" of *la grande hystérie*, as they were exhibited in the scenographic tableaux he staged. It was this typology which allowed him to connect hysteria to witchcraft, as it was depicted in paintings. But the explanatory part of his theory connected the bodily "poses" of the hysterics only to mysterious "organic lesions" of the cortex; sexuality was not a causal factor.

In this manner, he overcame the confusion of symptoms which had made hysteria emblematic of those mental disorders whose symptoms were a form of dissimilation or lying. But the staging of hysterical poses opened the possibility of a sort of counter-movement on the part of the hysterics: the possibility of disrupting the clear space of visibility, by introducing a sexual body. In this way, sexuality got into the picture. "I believe," Foucault said at the Collège de France in 1974, "that there was a *battle* of hysteria. . . . Hysteria was the set of phenomena of *struggle* that unfolded around this new medical machinery which was the neurological clinic."[38]

In the face of this sexual body, Charcot was obliged to turn away his "admirable gaze." Babinski gave up the theatricalization of the sickness and invented as an explanation "pithiatism," or the aptitude to let oneself be theatricalized. But Freud resolved to say, and to say theoretically, just what this space gave to be seen. The origin of hysteria, he said, lay in a woman's relation to her *sexuality*. And, around the theme of sexuality, Freud began to devise ways to connect what the hysteric *showed* with what she *said* in a new sort of space: the space of psychoanalysis.

With this sort of analysis, Foucault hoped to account for one feature that would distinguish the fascination and exhibition of sexuality in our society; one he sees Freud as having basically extended: its *medicalization*. What it is that we still want to see and to show about our sexual experience is its abnormality, its perversion, its sickness. And that fascination is an integral part of the pleasure we take in *knowing* about it.

One technology employed in Charcot's demonstrations was the new art of photography, and the photographs of the hysterical postures were published by the surrealists, who, as is well known, took a particular interest in the relation of seeing to mental disorder.

THE EYE OF THOUGHT

What is it then to see the events in what is unthought in our thought? One visual image Foucault offers is that of surrounding the event with a sort of "polyhedron of intelligibility," the sides of which would extend indefinitely in many directions.[39] It is to multiply the things associated with its "intelligibility," and the ways they are associated with it. The greater and more specific the internal conceptual analysis of the event, the greater the external processes with which its "invisible" or "evident" intelligibility is linked. Thus in Foucault's analysis of the event of the prison-form, he finds an intelligibility that connects it to pedagogical practices, professional armies, British empiricism, the new division of labor, and the invention of gunpowder, through the transference of technical models to other domains, new applications of theories, or new strategies to deal with local problems.

Foucault thus starts with the idea that there may be no such thing, no such "essence" as *the* visual, something that might be described by a "phenomenology of perception" or a "theory of the gaze," something which, following Martin Jay, Foucault would be against. Rather, history presents us with many different singular sorts of visual intelligibility, ways of seeing and making seeable, the unity of which is not to be found in the nature of the eye, empirical or transcendental, or in "the imaginary order." Where and when "the visual" acquires the status of essence, universality, and necessity, the philosopher's eye must look for the singular and contingent processes that make it self-evident, and so acceptable.

Something as in the philosophical task captured in Wittgenstein's famous precept "don't think, look!", the philosopher's eye, the eye of thought, is neither contemplative nor introspective. It does not look up to see the forms it has forgotten, or look within to see the point from which action should proceed, or the self-certainty from which knowledge should be derived.[40.] It looks *out* to those events in thought through which things are given to be seen. It looks out in order to *change* its way of seeing. Thus in 1981, Foucault declared:

> Each time I have attempted to do theoretical work it has been on the basis of elements from my experience—always in relations I *saw* taking place around me. It is in fact because I thought I recognized something cracked, dully jarring or dysfunctioning in the things I *saw*, in the institutions with which I dealt, in my relations with others, that I undertook a particular piece of work, several fragments of an autobiography.[41]

When a philosopher "sees" something problematic or dysfunctioning around him, he doesn't turn his eye around to the ideals in whose light the problems appear as imperfections or counter-instances; he doesn't turn it within to see the true or authentic self in whose light the problems figure as distortions or mystifications. His seeing starts a form of theoretical work which, in analyzing how the problems arose and were conceived, transforms his way of seeing them—and so his way of *living*.

ETHOS, BEAUTY, DANGER

"Fragments of an autobiography"—Foucault's art of seeing is also a philosophical art of living. His theoretical work is "autobiographical" not because it is a way of transcribing his experiences, but because it forms an exercise in which to periodically question the given conceptions of his experience, and so look for new ones. Autobiography in this sense is not the attempt to provide an image or picture of who one was or how one should be seen, but a form of work to change oneself by changing one's way of seeing.

Foucault's writings do not unfold as a single doctrine or theory of things. At particular moments he changed his mind as to his aims, objects, and methods. As in the case of Nietzsche, Wittgenstein, or Heidegger, his thought is punctuated by transformations in the way he conceived of his own philosophical task. In the Introduction to the volumes published shortly before his death, he pictures this process as an exercise or *ascesis* of disengaging himself from himself in his work *(se déprendre de soi-même)*, through "essays" that try to alter his way of seeing things. But he adds, there is an irony in this process. It is precisely such efforts to free oneself from oneself that makes one's work one's own; one finds who one has been by always getting away from oneself.

> Such is the irony of the efforts one makes to change one's way of seeing *(façon de voir)*. . . . Have they in fact led to thinking in another way *(penser autrement)?* Maybe at best they have allowed one to think in another way what one already thought, and to see what one has done from a different vantage point and in a clearer light. . . .

And the new light under which Foucault saw what he had been doing in his previous work was the light of "problematizations":

> I now feel I better perceive how . . . I was proceeding in this enterprise of a history of truth: to analyze . . . the *problematizations* through which being gives itself as what can be, and what must be, thought, and the *practices* through which these *problematizations* are formed.[42]

There may be no final "enlightened" solution to our relations with pain, illness, crime, madness, and death. And yet it is a historical fact that there arose various forms of intelligibility or rationality in the way people actually came to see such things, and the way they consequently erected around themselves forms of knowledge and action, and modes of living. Those experiences have not always been seen as raising the same sorts of problems. To analyze their history is to see the specific sorts of danger or problem which led to the evidence of a particular way of conceiving and dealing with them. Thus, according to his new way of seeing, what he would have been studying, in his previous work, is how people *saw* what is dangerous in being mad, ill, or criminal, how they envisaged those dangers and made them "visible" or "spatialized" them in knowledge and action.

Foucault proposed to view his histories of madness, of illness, or of crime as histories of just what it was in the experience of madness, illness, or crime which was so problematic as to become something which both could be, and *had* to be thought. And he began to associate such problematizations of experience with particular modes of living or being, modes of being a person of a particular sort. Thus he would have been asking what are the problematizations and consequent practices "by which man proposes to think his own nature when he perceives himself to be mad; when he considers himself to be ill; when he conceives of himself as a living, speaking, laboring being; when he judges himself as a criminal?"[43]

In the *Birth of the Clinic*, Foucault had looked for something more basic than the "mindless phenomenologies" of the "encounter" between doctor and patient, and the "so-called 'liberal'" notion of a contract or pact between two individuals. He had tried to see a "major event in the relations of man to himself and to the language of things."[44] The new "spatialization" of illness in the pathologies of the individual organs would have fundamentally changed the relations people had to themselves and to one another in "being ill." It would introduce a whole new sort of "ethical" intelligibility of the problems of doctor, patient, and pathologist.

Similarly, Foucault's history of madness may be read as an examination of how "being mad" was seen as a source of danger in society and in the individual. Thus there arose a new way of seeing the problem of madness. The class of inmates in the General Hospital may seem heteroclite to us. It answered to a perfectly intelligible way of seeing a problem, a "sensibility" for which the central danger to society and self had become *idleness*. This way of seeing derived in part from a theological promotion of idleness over vanity as the cardinal sin. It also arose from a new conception of labor and poverty that was to become the target of a new administrative sort of rationality. And it was central in the thinking through which the hysteria of idle women could enter medical discourse.

But as the techniques of moral assignation in the "enlightened" asylums of Tuke and Pinel show, there arose a question not simply of dangers from without, or in social relations, but also from within, or in one's relation to oneself, and so to others. Guilt, shame, irresponsibility, weakness of the will as forms of relations to one's self arise within different spaces and under different conceptions; they are conceived in relation to particular dangers or problems.[45]

The new light of problematization thus brought into focus the *ethical* concerns of his previous histories. It offered Foucault a way of thinking about the origins and the changes in the very conception of ethics: its basic questions, what it supposed to be true about us, the sorts of relations it was thought to have with knowledge law, or politics.

To be sure, Foucault had not been worried about the justification of the principles of ethical action; rather, he had been studying how ethical thought and practice had seen and responded to certain sorts of problems or dangers: the ways *it* had conceived of the obstacles one must overcome to be good or do right, the ways *it* had rationalized a way of dealing with what it saw as wrong, sinful, or evil.

The possibility of a history of ethics arose that would study the specific sorts of dangers or problems it was designed to overcome. But, in studying this history, we should not look "for the solution of a current problem in the solution another problem raised at another moment by other people." The history of the problematizations of "ways of being" in ethics is not a nostalgic one. "History," Foucault said, "protects us from historicism—from the historicism that calls on the past to respond to questions of the present." [46]

Rather, Foucault says, the analysis of problematizations is itself "dangerous." In the *Order of Things*, Foucault had already said that when, in modern thinking, the "cosmological" form of moral thought is no longer possible, it is thought itself which becomes dangerous —a "perilous act." [47] And, speaking of his "pessimistic activism" in a late interview, Foucault declared: "I would like to do the genealogy of problems, of *problématiques*. My point is not that everything is bad, but that everything is dangerous, which is not the same thing as bad. If everything is dangerous, then we always have something to do." [48]

In his last work, and in his last conception of his work, Foucault connected his art of seeing to the "ethico-political choice" one makes of "determining which is the real danger." The choice of trying to see just what it is that we have to struggle against in order to free ourselves (and free ourselves *from* ourselves). And this freedom is dangerous, since we can never have in advance a determinant or complete picture of it.

For, as a thinker and seer, Foucault was concerned with a situation, prior to the possibility of deductive normative reasoning, where one sees something must be done without yet knowing what. A space not of deduction but of questioning and analysis is thus opened up between the choice one makes and what one does, in which one tries to conceive what the danger is which one does not yet fully see, but in relation to which one must take action. It is one's responsibility to this thing that troubles, but which one can't yet describe or name, that requires one to work to change oneself.

One's work is the attempt to change one's way of seeing and living in relation to those specific dangers one does not yet know what to do about.

Foucault thought that this kind of relation between seeing, living, and action might be conceived as an "aesthetics of existence" which contrasted with the one he tried to reconstruct in the ancient ethical schools of *savoir-vivre*.

In Foucault's reconstruction of ancient ethical thought, what in sex was seen as dangerous enough to become the object of a whole practice of self-transformation was not yet the sins of the flesh or the odd desires that fascinate us and that lurk in the pathogenic recesses of our heads. It was the excessive activity that threatened a loss of self-mastery in those meant to rule—a danger to the *ethos*, the fitting mode of being, of the free adult male. But the *ethos* of the "civic man" in his health, home, and courtship, around which the ancient ethical practices turned, was rather different from the ethos of the Christian "inward man," and the Augustinian problem that all sexual desire is tinged by the Fall, and is the model of sin in general, or the "democracy of shame" that linked the Christian community to the problem of poverty. Foucault sought to analyze these great changes in the problems of "being sexual" in terms of the ethical practices in which one is asked to transform oneself under a particular conception of one's experience, aims, and obligations.

In the analysis of the ancient arts of being virtuous, seeing and being seen played a significant role. As has often been observed, the ancient conception of "beauty"—beauty in the ethical sense—was a particularly *visual* one. And yet such activities of "presentation of self" were "problematized" and conceived in a rather different manner from the questions of identity, authenticity, and engagement Sartre associated with "the gaze." If the proud virile body of the master was a "lived body," it was lived in a different way than the one Sartre had envisaged in his account of our "concrete relations" with ourselves and one another. Seeing oneself and one's mode of living had a different sort of intelligibility in this ethics.

Self-mastery was like the visualized evidence of one's fitness to rule. One had to be able to show, and to show *truly*, one's state of temperate control of soul and body as something noble and beautiful to be glorified for posterity. The aim or telos of the self-forming practices was thus a beautiful accord or harmony between who one is and what one does and says. Beauty was an ethical category;

seeing and showing oneself were thus part of an etho-poetics, an aesthetics of existence. And the link between visible beauty and mode of being took place and was formed in certain "spaces," the *oikos*, and the *agora*. The *oikos* was a "space of constructed visibility." Discussion of marital duties was a discussion of the distribution of roles and natures in the "space" of the *oikos*, whose "roof" divided what was inside from outside. Thus there was the problem of makeup and paint in a debate about pleasures and truth: makeup can have no place in the beautiful way the mistress of the house must "carry herself," in which "standing and walking will give her body that certain demeanor, that carriage *(allure)* which, in the eyes of the Greeks, characterized the figure *(la plastique)* of the free individual."[49] In this idea of beauty, *mimesis* was a category at once of one's relation to oneself, or one's "figure," and of the relation of the "figure" of a work to what it makes appear.

If Hegel saw in this Greek experience of beauty a first "moment" of that to which spirit returns in the work of history which passes through art and religion to the state, for Foucault, the Greek experience is rather a "lost evidence," a solution to a danger no longer ours. The art of making oneself in the image of an active freedom no longer has the same central and self-evident place in our ethical thought. We have lost the "ethopoetics" that made existence the object of an aesthetics. We see other dangers, and deal with them in other ways. Our disciplined "docile and useful" bodies are not the "self-possessed" bodies of the ancient master. The Benthamite spaces which helped give the calculability of what is good for us its central ethical importance are rather different from the spaces in which the ancient question of the wisdom of the good life was raised.

For there to be a modern "aesthetics of existence," the very concept of beauty in living must change. This is the change Foucault associated with Baudelaire, and with the modern principle that "the subject is not given." For us the danger is not that we might fail to become what we are meant to be, but that we might only be what we can see ourselves to be. In ancient thought, freedom was something beautiful to be made visible in soul and body; and the loss of freedom could thus be seen as something ugly. But when "the subject is not given," our freedom ceases to have an image. It is that which we can never yet see. Its beauty lies in this danger. For us, beauty no longer resides in the perfection of a living harmony between ourselves and the "spaces" in which we can become what it is natural, given, and possible for us to be, but in what cannot yet be seen or named about us in the spaces we inhabit.

Beauty in living would lie in a dissonance or disharmony between one's given nature and one's possibilities of existence, between one's identity and what one can see in oneself and in the processes going on around one. The danger of beauty thus gives rise to an *oeuvre de soi* in which to see what one should do is to change one's mode of living, and in which changing one's mode of living involves changing one's way of seeing, one's *façon de voir*. One changes oneself as one comes to see what is dangerous in one's existence, and comes to see what is dangerous by changing oneself.

Foucault thus came to think of the art of seeing he had been practicing as an "aesthetics of existence," an art of living. In this art, the events one sees going on around one interrupt one's sense of one's self and cause one to think and to rethink. Foucault's exercise in seeing and thinking would then be the exercise for a modern *ethos* of freedom—the freedom for which we never yet have the image and the ethos in which beauty lies in coming to see the real dangers we must face.

SEEING OUTSIDE

This attempt to move out from oneself in the "essays" one writes is not so unlike the "attitude to modernity" Foucault finds in Baudelaire. In the course of a late discussion of Kant's paper on enlightenment, he says that Baudelaire's "exercise on himself" as a writer would transpire in "another, different place," outside the realm of society and politics—the place Baudelaire called "art."[50] How, then, is Foucault's "art of seeing" related to the way he saw this "art"? And, in particular, what does this "art of seeing" have to do with the conception of "modern" art and literature, which he himself advanced in a series of essays in the '60s, but from which he later sought to distance himself? It is important for Deleuze's reading to establish a continuity throughout Foucault's work based in his early conception of work or oeuvre.

In the last pages of *Madness and Civilization*, one can already find the germs of this question in the discussion of *absence d'oeuvre*, a post-Romantic idea with roots in Sade and Hölderlin, in which one's relation to madness would be linked to one's oeuvre not as its expressive content, but as the unsayable or unspeakable source from which the work would emerge, and into which it would again disappear.[51] *"Absence d'oeuvre"* doesn't mean there is no work or that one is out of work, as the English translations oddly suggest.[52] Rather through one's work one tries to say something as yet unsayable, or to see something as yet invisible, and so one opens out a space of a sort of rhythmic "disappearance" of oneself in and through one's work. The "being of language" (as distinct from its regulated use in "discourse") would offer the occasion and the condition of this modern "attitude" to oneself in one's work. In the '60s Foucault argued that this was a conception basic to the work of such writers as Klossowski, Bataille, and Blanchot.

English-language discussion has mostly ignored this theme in Foucault's own oeuvre. And yet it is the one Derrida admired in his critical review of Foucault. It is also the one which Deleuze invokes in another way in his presentation of Foucault as seer. In effect, he sees Foucault as bringing the exercise of writing as *désoeuvrement* into the fields of history, politics, and epistemology. Deleuze says the "being of language," which would be the condition and occasion of literature is also the condition and occasion of Foucault's archeology of discourse. And he says the opening of visibility, or "the being of light," which would be the chance of the visual arts, is also the condition of Foucault's art of seeing.[53]

That is one reason Deleuze can say that Foucault is "singularly close to film." For the central concept in Deleuze's own analysis of the role of thought in film is the concept of *désoeuvrement*. In response to Godard's prognostication of an end to film theory, he says "the concepts of film are not given in film."[54] There is a sort of "filmic unthought" from which film tries constantly to free itself and so open itself to other ways of thinking and showing. Thought in film is a *tout ouvert*, a conceptual ensemble open to transformation. As such it can be analyzed as a great art of conceiving of light, movement, time, and space, of conceptualizing the visuality of the "spaces" through which we are given to be seen. Deleuze contests the attempt of Christian Metz to make narrative the central question around which filmic thought must turn, and the resulting choice one would have to make between the good abstract or theoretical film, and the bad commercial, ideological, narrative one. The visuality films make intelligible is not that of the physical medium theory must purify of all *récit;* it is a tacit conceptual organization which links film to the way of space, subjectivity, and time are philosophically understood.

And yet, after '68, or with his "political" turn, one hears a good deal less about the "being of language" (or of light) in Foucault's work, and the figures of Nietzsche, Hölderlin, and Bataille cease to haunt the margins of his institutional histories. As I say in my book, Foucault changes his mind about Sade and Bataille. And in a posthumously published interview from 1975, Foucault himself says as much.[55] He says that in his essays on such figures as Blanchot and Bataille in the '60s, it was not the idea of literature itself which was important to him. The reference to such figures in his histories, he says, was a matter of simple *constat*, something he would have noted in passing as though on a walk. What was important to him in Blanchot was the attempt to get out of a certain "Hegelianism" that assigned literature a privileged expressive role in history, and to ask instead about the singular place a society would accord to the writing it calls literary. Blanchot was one way out of a certain style of philosophy; it offered the possibility of another way of thinking in which one tries constantly to see outside the bounds of seeing and think outside the bounds of thinking. But at the same time, Foucault says he came to adopt a "negative attitude" toward the "sacralization" of this new conception of literature which took hold in the university, a sacralization, which, paradoxically, this new literature had first intended to resist. He says there arose an "ultra-rationalist" and "ultra-lyrical" idea of a literature radical in referring only to itself, in which writing would acquire inviolable rights to "subversion," and in which the more involuted one could make one's writing, the more "revolutionary" one would become. Foucault saw this idea as a form of "political blockage," and presents his own books on Roussel and Rivière as his way out of the new academic sanctification of literature.

Nevertheless, one can argue that his early ideas about the oeuvres of modernity did not altogether disappear from his thinking. If *absence d'oeuvre* ceases to be an object of his histories, it comes to supply something of the *ethos* of his work as historian. Rather than being the obscure hero of his histories, Nietzsche would be someone he would put to a new *use;* and he would continue Baudelaire's "attitude to modernity" in his own work in another way. It is thus that Foucault would extend the place Baudelaire called "art" to a particular ethic of thinking, seeing, and living.

In "La pensée du dehors," Foucault speaks of an "absence" that would not be *in* an oeuvre, but would be its outside, its *dehors*. He says modernist literature is not the literature that turns in on itself, but which opens itself outside itself. It does not try to make beautiful forms appear within it, but transports those forms outside what they have seen. *Le dehors* is not the "external world"—the "world outside the text"—but the world it is not yet possible to see or to foresee. For as it occurs, it changes what we can and cannot see; it is the possibility of another way of seeing in the history of what we see.[56]

In this sense Foucault's art of seeing might be said to be the art of seeing outside ourselves, or seeing the "absence" in our work. Not to look within to a true or authentic self; not to master one's time by holding it in one's thought; not to find a place for oneself within society or state, but to look out from oneself, to open one's time to what has not yet been seen, to transform or displace one's instituted, assigned identity at a time and place. In this sense Foucault's art of seeing is an art of looking out, which would "give new impetus, as far and wide as possible, to the undefined work of freedom."[57]

NOTES

1. Gilles Deleuze, *Foucault* (Paris: Editions Minuit, 1986), p. 57; English translation (Minneapolis: University of Minnesota Press, 1989). One might trace an original view of "vision" in Deleuze's readings of philosophers. Thus, for example, in the '60s, he also presents Spinoza, philosopher and lens-polisher, as a *vivant-voyant*. Spinoza said that the geometrical demonstrations of his *Ethics* were as "the eyes of the soul"; Deleuze sees a vital optical method of rectifying those sad passions that ruin life, a way of polishing the glass for an inspired free vision. Deleuze's latest book is about Leibniz and the Baroque.

2. *Ibid.*, p. 59.

3. *Ibid.*, p. 72.

4. In an essay entitled "In the Empire of the Gaze: Foucault and the Denigration of Vision in Twentieth-Century French Thought," in *Foucault: A Critical Reader*, David Hoy, ed. (London: Basil Blackwell, 1986), Martin Jay offers a useful inventory of some of the places where Foucault discusses matters visual. But I would disagree with what he takes to be the central theme of the discussion—"the denigration of vision." On my reading, to say that Panoptic architecture or surveillance is a "diagram" of one kind of power is not to be against vision, or even to take vision as central (as in what Jay terms "oculo-centrism"). I am not sure just what Jay means by "vision" or "the visual," and what it would mean to "denigrate" it. I think that Foucault did not take "the visual" as a single thing, and that his questioning of specific kinds of seeing was not at all a rejection of seeing as such. I take Foucault rather as a critical historian of the *events* of seeing, of what we can and cannot see at a time and place.

97

5. It would be interesting to study in what ways *Annales* historians have come in fact to contribute to period films. In "Anti-Rétro," Foucault discusses such films as *Lacombe Lucien* and *The Night Porter* in relation to the "rétro-style in clothes and home decoration. His analysis of the return to previous styles is neither that of "simulation" or empty recycling, nor that of anamnesis (*Cahiers du Cinéma*, July 1974).

6. Michel Foucault, *Discipline and Punish*, Alan Sheridan, trans. (New York: Pantheon, 1977), p. 228.

7. Deleuze, *Foucault*, p. 65.

8. I contrast Freud's view of dreaming with that of Artemidorus, as discussed by Foucault in *The Care of the Self* (John Rajchman, "Ethics after Foucault," *Socialtext*, Winter 1985). In his early introduction to his translation of Binswanger's *Dream and Existence, Review of Existential Psychology and Psychiatry* (1984–85), vol. 9, no. 1, Foucault objects to Freud that he reduces the dream to the dream-report. But in his mature work the visuality of dreaming is understood in historical rather than existential terms.

9. See the remarks in *Technologies of the Self: A Seminar with Michel Foucault* (Amherst: University of Massachusetts Press, 1988), p. 14: "What I react against is the fact that there is a breach between social history and the history of ideas. Social historians are supposed to describe how people act without thinking, and historians of ideas are supposed to describe how people think without acting. Everybody both acts and thinks. The way people act or react is linked to a way of thinking, and, of course, thinking is related to tradition."

The idea of *visibilités* is that how people act and react when they see something is made possible by a particular way of thinking related to tradition. One might understand in this light the project Foucault announced in the last pages of the *Archeology of Knowledge* to study painting as a "discursive practice" rather than seeing it as "pure vision that must be inscribed into the materiality of space," or as "naked gesture," or as "always a way of saying." In Michel Foucault, *The Archeology of Knowledge*, A. M. Sheridan Smith, trans. (New York: Harper & Row, 1976), pp. 193–194. Painting would be "shot through with positivity"; the self-evident character of its "visuality" would derive from a materially rooted way of thinking. Thought would make one particular kind of visuality seem natural or essential to painting. To study such "positivity" would consist in asking how the concepts were brought together under which paintings could be seen, where, by what means, by whom, and so forth.. Through what "system of thought" were the "objects" of painting, the class of things that could be painted, specified? And how was this delimitation connected to the spaces in which it could be seen (church or chateau, gallery or museum) and those in which it came to be made (studio, academy, etc.) and so to the legal and economic rules that governed its ownership and its circulation? In what way was the mode of "being a painter" conceived?

How did technological innovations become part of the rationality or intelligibility of the "techniques" open to painting? How did the "materiality" of painting become more than the "context" in which it was seen or made, part of the way it was conceived (as when Foucault says that Manet was the first museum painter)? And in which ways was this construction of the conceptual space of painting linked to other or associated fields in the thinking of the age? To study thus the "events of the visual" in the history of painting would suppose that people are much less free to paint than they think, that there is much more conceptual "regularity" in the practice of painting than they imagine; but since that regularity is also what opens painting to change and transformation, people are much more free to paint than they imagine.

10. Ian Hacking, *The Emergence of Probability* (Cambridge: Cambridge University Press, 1975).

11. Foucault, *L'Impossible Prison*, Michelle Perrot, ed. (Paris, Seuil, 1980), p. 44.

12. Foucault, *The Birth of the Clinic*, A. M. Sheridan Smith, trans. (New York: Vintage Books, 1975), p. 3.

13. Foucault, *Discipline and Punish*, p. 232.

14. *Ibid.* In *The Use of Pleasure*, Foucault also says, "I wanted first to dwell on that quite recent and banal notion of 'sexuality': to stand detached from it, *to get around its familiar self-evidence (contourner son évidence familière)* . . . it was a matter of *seeing* how an 'experience' came to be constituted in modern Western societies . . ." *The Use of Pleasure*, Robert Hurley, trans. (New York: Random House, 1985), pp. 3–4. Translation revised and emphasis added.

15. In the "Eye of Power," referring to the work of Jean Starobinski, Foucault briefly alludes to the Rousseauistic dream of a transparent society. In *Power/Knowledge* (New York: Pantheon, 1980), pp. 152–153.

16. "An Interview with Gilles Deleuze," *History of the Present* (Spring 1986), p. 1.

17. *Ibid.*

18. *Foucault/Blanchot* (New York: Zone Books, 1987), p. 24.

19. Foucault, *The Use of Pleasure*, p. 9.

20. Foucault, *ibid.*, p. 218.

21. Richard Rorty, *Philosophy and the Mirror of Nature* (Princeton: Princeton University Press, 1979).

22. Foucault, *The Order of Things* (New York: Pantheon, 1970), p. 43.

23. It would be the same "separation of the eye" that characterizes the classical primacy of observation in knowledge, which would characterize the classical primacy of perception in painting. The tradition of *ut pictura poesis* would be challenged by saying that painting employs a different sort of sign, or has a different form, from poetry; it would be given to the eye alone, not to the ear. There would emerge an examination of this form through which painting presents itself to the perceiving eye, which

would permit the criticism of paintings to be distinguished from their "commentary." This classical distinction between criticism and commentary, or between form and content, would then initiate a long debate Foucault here sees Mallarmé as changing. Foucault, *The Order of Things*, pp. 78–87.

24. Clement Greenberg's "formalism" is "classical" in this sense. He even cites Lessing in his attempt to find the principle of the turn to abstraction in modern painting in a process by which each of the "classical" arts would turn to the specific problems of its "medium." Such would be the secret of the isolation of "form" central to the avant-garde's attempt to preserve the "value" of art in an age of kitsch and socialist realism. In thus making the physical medium the privileged object of visual intelligence, Greenberg thought he had discovered the *essence* of the visuality or optically of the visual arts. Historically, this essence was rooted in the classical self-evidence of painting as a perceived object; and there is a self-declared *positivism* in Greenberg's account of abstraction in modern art. What now seems invisible in Greenberg's conception of the essence of the visual is precisely the famous "eye" of the formalist critics that has learned to see only forms, and the way that eye was transferred to painter or sculptor as an obligation to "purify" his visual intelligence by seeing his object in "purely" formal terms. What that eye could not "see" was the other *conception* of the visual found in Duchamp, dadaism, and surrealism. On this point, see Rosalind Krauss on the optical unconscious; in "The Blink of an Eye," David Carroll, ed., *"The States of 'Theory"* (New York: Columbia University Press, 1989). Thierry de Duve contrasts the essentiality of Greenberg's conception of the avant-garde with the "pictorial nominalism" of the Duchampian avant-garde, where the question of how the visual is itself to be named or conceived becomes a central artistic problem. In *Le nominalism pictural* (Paris: Editions Minuit, 1984).

25. Foucault, *The Order of Things*, p. 43.

26. See the discussion of science and ideology in *The Archeology of Knowledge*, pp. 184–186.

27. In his *Michel Foucault and the History of Reason* (Cambridge: Cambridge University Press, forthcoming) Gary Gutting presents a clear and detailed account of Canguilhem's distinction between the history of concepts and the history of theories. His book is a good corrective to the view that Foucault was against objectivity or rationality.

28. Foucault, *Discipline and Punish*, pp. 185, 184.

29. Ian Hacking, *Representing and Intervening* (Cambridge: Cambridge University Press, 1983).

30. Foucault, *Archeology of Knowledge*, p. 47.

31. Foucault, *Discipline and Punish*, p. 171.

32. *Ibid.*, p. 226.

33. Foucault, "The Eye of Power," *Knowledge/Power*, pp. 149–150.

34. Hoy, ed., *Foucault Reader*, p. 86.

35. Foucault, *The History of Sexuality*, Robert Hurley, trans. (New York: Pantheon, 1978), p. 86.

36. *Ibid.*, p. 71.

37. *Ibid.*, pp. 55–57.

38. Quoted in Jacques Lagrange, "Versions de la psychanalyse dans le texte de Foucault," in *Psychanalyse à l'Université* (April 1987), p. 263. In "The Ethics of Care for the Self as a Practice of Freedom," in *Philosophy and Social Criticism* (Summer 1987), 12:122, Foucault says that hysteria strikes him as the "very illustration" of a struggle of being constituted as mad: "It is not altogether a coincidence that the important phenomena of hysteria have been studied exactly where there was a maximum of coercion to compel individuals to consider themselves mad."

39. Deleuze says Foucault's "conception of the visible seems pictorial, close to Delaunay, for whom light . . . created its own forms and its own movements." Delaunay said "Cézanne broke the fruit dish, and we should not glue it together again, as the cubists do." See also *Image-Temps*, where Deleuze has similar things to say about the non-expressionist use of light in the films of Rivette. *L'Image-Temps* (Paris: Editions Minuit, 1985), pp. 20ff. This is, of course, not the only way of connecting Foucault's art of seeing to modern pictorial practices.

40. Foucault briefly discusses Plato's "famous metaphor of the eye," in Hoy, ed., *Foucault Reader*, pp. 367–368.

41. Foucault, "Est-il donc important de penser?" *Libération*, May 30–31, 1981.

42. Foucault, *The Use of Pleasure*, p. 11 (translation revised).

43. *Ibid.* p. 7.

44. Foucault, *The Birth of the Clinic*, p. xiv.

45. In his *L'Etat Providence* (Paris: Grasset, 1986), François Ewald argues that accidents constituted a new sort of danger or problem, which, for example, does not figure in the sort of catalogue of the evils of the eighteenth century one finds in Voltaire's *Candide*. With the insurance strategy used to administer the risks of accidents emerged a new sort of "juridical experience" and a new class of rights.

46. Hoy, ed., *Foucault Reader*, pp. 343 and 250.

47. Foucault, *The Order of Things*, p. 328.

48. Hoy, ed., *Foucault Reader*, p. 343.

49. Foucault, *The Use of Pleasure*, p. 162. In "The Ethics of Care for the Self as a Practice of Freedom," Foucault says, "The Greeks, in fact, considered . . . the freedom of the individual as an ethical problem. But ethical in the sense that the Greeks could understand. *Ethos* was the deportment and the way to behave. It was the subject's mode of being and a certain manner of acting *visible to others*. One's *ethos was seen* by his dress, by his bearing, by his gait, by the poise with which he reacts to events, etc. For them that is the concrete expression of liberty. That is the way they 'problematized' their freedom" (p. 117, emphasis added).

50. Hoy, ed., *Foucault Reader*, p. 42.

51. Foucault, *Madness and Civilization*, Richard Howard, trans. (New York: Vintage Books, 1973), pp. 229ff.

52. Richard Howard's "the absence of the work of art" would translate *L'absence de l'oeuvre* not *L'absence d'oeuvre*. Alan Sheridan thinks the term means "an unproductive idleness, outside human achievement." In Alan Sheridan, *Foucault: The Will to Truth* (London: Tavistock, 1980), p. 15.

53. Deleuze tends to pair "discursivity" with words and concepts and "visibility" with things and intuitions or sensibilities. But, according to another reading of Foucault's idiom, one can "say" things with images and space just as one can "show" things with words or sentences. Language is one way of "spatializing" or "visualizing," and there are "evidences" of discourses just as there are of "sensibilities." Conversely spaces or images can make statements. Thus, for example, just as much as the letters on the typewriter keyboard, it might count as an *énoncé* that, during the colonial period, maps were made with Britain at the center. Perhaps the relation between ways of seeing and ways of saying in Foucault lies in the histories of the tacit thinking that underlies them, and does not easily match with the traditional distinctions between concept and intuition, or word and thing.

54. Deleuze, *L'Image-Temps*, p. 365.

55. "Foucault, passe-frontières de la philosophie," *Le Monde*, September 6, 1986.

56. The theme of *l'absence d'oeuvre* plays a complex role in the response to Foucault in the work of Jacques Derrida. In "Cogito et histoire de la folie," Derrida declares, "Now, madness is in essence what is not said *(ce qui ne se dit pas)*: it is *l'absence d'oeuvre* Foucault says profoundly" (*Ecriture et différence*, p. 68). But the discussion does not end there, Derrida's essay "Comment ne pas parler" may be read as a more complex reflection on the senses of "absence" as "what is not said." His discussion of negative theology in this essay has much in common with Foucault's short treatment of it in *La Pensée du dehors*. Both essays concern the problem of *space*. But Derrida returns to the theme of *l'absence d'oeuvre* in his recent writings on architecture. He questions a still negative-theological sense of "absence" in the writings and work of Eisenman and Liebeskind. And he says this about Tschumi's *Folies:* "Of these follies, then, these follies in every sense, we say, *for once*, that they do not lead to ruin, the ruin of defeat or the ruin of nostalgia. They are not the same as *l'absence d'oeuvre*—that destiny of *madness in the classic age* of which Foucault spoke. They make work, they put to work. *(Elles font oeuvre, elles mettent en oeuvre)*" (*Psyché*, Paris: Galilée, 1987, p. 481). I think both Foucault and Derrida would agree that the question of *l'absence d'oeuvre* is the question of *events*. See "What's New in Architecture," below.

57. Hoy, ed., *Foucault Reader*, p. 46.

Part III

THE HISTORY OF A CATEGORY

FIVE

The Postmodern Museum

"Les Immatériaux" (March 28–July 25, 1985) was the most expensive exhibition in the Beaubourg museum to date. A collective effort of more than fifty people working over two years under the auspices of the Centre de Création Industrielle, it was directed by the French philosopher Jean-François Lyotard. Lyotard and company transformed the fifth floor of the museum into a gigantic metallic maze, divided by gray gauze screens into sixty-one "sites"; these sites were arranged consecutively along five adjacent pathways. For the most part the sites consisted of small installations of various cultural artifacts; technological representations and electronic devices, and were titled by the ideas or conditions that they were intended to represent or demonstrate.

The visitor entered the maze equipped with headphones that furnished a sound track synchronized with the sites—a selection of dramatically recited classics mostly from French theory (Blanchot, Baudrillard, Barthes) and modern writing (Beckett, Artaud, Mallarmé, Proust, Zola, Kleist). In this manner one confronted an extraordinary array of things taken from hospitals, factories, re-

This article first appeared in *Art in America* (October 1985) and is reprinted here by permission of *Art in America*.

search centers, libraries, and museums of all sorts—from Paris' Musée national d'art moderne to the Center of Creative Photography at the University of Arizona. IBM and astrophysics laboratories were credited along with well-known artists. Most European countries were represented, as well as Japan, the United States, and Australia; there was little, however, from the third world.

There were video, film, slides and photographs—commercial and artistic, anonymous and signed, old and recent. There were robots, an elaborate photocopier, the first display of a holographic movie, and, of course, computers—lots of them. There were examples of rugosymmetric reproduction, electromicroscopy, spectrography, holography, Doppler effects, and Fourier series; displays of astrophysics, genetics, and statistics. There was even a Japanese sleeping cell from the Kotobuki Seating Co.

Works of art—traditional, modernist, and Conceptual—were juxtaposed with technological displays or ludic devices to make music or compose poems. Among the artists and authors variously represented in the sites were Hans Christian Andersen and Jacques Derrida, Georges Seurat and Elvis Costello, Joseph Kosuth and Edgar Allan Poe, Malevich and Muybridge, Moholy-Nagy and Saul Steinberg, Robert Ryman and Peter Eisenman, Duchamp and Warhol, Yves Klein and Irving Penn. At several computer consoles positioned throughout the show one could read the meditations of thirty illustrious Parisian intellectuals and writers on fifty alphabetized and cross-referenced words such as Author, Desire, Meaning, Mutation, Simulation, Voice, and Speed. "Les Immatériaux" boasted many great names; but not only were things not classified by such proper names, one was told (explicitly by Derrida in a text set near the beginning of the show) that "authorship" itself was in question.

Yet while all these heteroclite objects figured in sites titled by the concepts they were supposed to illustrate, the aim of the show was not the didactic one of presenting new art work or new technical devices to the public. Rather, the objective was to induce a state of uncertainty, an inability to name what it is that all these sites might refer to. "That we know not how to name what awaits us is the sure sign that it awaits us,"[1] says Lyotard darkly to French *Vogue*. "Les Immatériaux" was intended not to be futurological, but to frustrate the demand to say what the future is—a future which surrounds us without our being able to name it, which is "ours," without our knowing how or why.

Two notions seemed to govern the conception of the show: "immateriality," implicit in the title, and "postmodernism," a particular concern of Lyotard the philosopher. How did these neologisms relate to this singular assemblage of objects? Was the show about a great reclassification, a new "order of things," that of postmodernism? Or is the postmodern condition rather like a Borgesian encyclopedia, a purposeless or random accumulation, a vast, overwhelming *bricolage*? These are like the questions of the Sphinx: who are you among all this? The show produced a plethora of supporting materials, explanations, and interviews, plus an international colloquium and an elaborate bibliography. And yet, when asked (in a *Flash Art* interview) what on earth postmodernism is, Lyotard responds with cunning modesty: "My work is, in fact, directed to finding out what it is, but I still don't know."[2]

THE INVERTED MUSEUM

"Les Immatériaux" was a singular museological exercise—the movement of an influential strand of current French thought into a museum space, a great public or popular display of what that thought takes to be our condition. We have seen "theoretical" artifacts, and art for theory's sake. Here it was the museum itself which was turned into a theoretical object.

Museums contextualize things. Not so many years back, pre-Beaubourg Cultural Minister André Malraux was talking about the "museum without walls." Today, any artifact becomes a putative museum object, something that might be acquired or appropriated by a museum without regard for its source or context. This museological process reached a sort of inverted apotheosis in "Les Immatériaux." The show included many "anti-aesthetic" artworks (e.g. Raoul Hausmann's *Spirit of Our Time, Mechanical Head*, 1919) once intended to challenge the spread of museological representation, and many readymade bits of "reality" once supposed to interrupt representation and so question "art." But today readymades are often considered high art, and it is "reality" which is questioned by a groundless multiplication of images. If our world is basically populated less by things than by simulacra, if everything exists only to be endlessly recomposed, the distinction between representation and reality seems to become irrelevant or "immaterial." "Les Immatériaux" addressed this state of affairs by suggesting a new continuity between what is inside and outside the museum:

107

the museum became no longer a space or sanctuary apart from things, but a mirror of their infinite reiteration.

It is to the French sociologist Jean Baudrillard that we owe the vision of a culture of simulacra, a culture of empty recycling of past contents. And it is precisely in the Beaubourg museum that he thinks this culture finds its monument and instrument. For Baudrillard, the postmodern condition is the Beaubourgeois condition. It is paradoxical to ask what to put into the museum, for the museum "functions as an incinerator absorbing and devouring all cultural energy"; to put nothing in it would be a Romantic gesture. Rather, one should accelerate the processes of simulation by turning the place into a "labyrinth, the infinite combinatory library . . . in short, the universe of Borges."[3] "Les Immatériaux" made this sardonic suggestion good; it even had the recorded voice of Baudrillard telling of the advent of the Age of the Simulacrum.

The modern museum recontextualizes things in a formal or aesthetic space. The postmodern museum, as intimated by the show, foregrounds the condition in which real and simulated things seem equivalent—an environment in which aesthetic, non-aesthetic, and even anti-aesthetic objects coexist. The museum of "Les Immatériaux" might be the first postmodern museum: it not only collected readymades from the most diverse sources; it set them within a universe of museological nominalism—there existed no fixed, general classification of things, no cultural division tied down by "Reality" or "Human Nature"; things were not compartmentalized into art and technology, high and mass cultures, esthetic and nonesthetic forms.

One inferred: "postmodern" culture does not affirm itself through a dominant art; it is not the sort of thing a cultural ministry can administrate. Its "ism" does not refer to a school with specific aesthetic principles; it has no manifesto or slogan or formal program. It does not justify itself with a progressive scheme; it sees the very idea of "advanced art" as one more arbitrary classification. In short, it has no "meta-narrative" to tell about itself. "Postmodern" refers instead to a condition, and "Les Immatériaux" was an attempt to dramatize that condition. What sort of drama was it? It was not narrative; it was not even disruptive in a Brechtian sense. It was electronic. The headphoned masses milling through the maze were part of it. When they made music with the motion of their bodies or composed poetry on a computer, there was no effect of "distance" or "alienation." One could not "participate" in this theater because one was already part of it.

THE PHILOSOPHER OF POSTMODERN LIFE

The master trope of "Les Immatériaux" derived from the Borges fable about the library that contains, in all conceivable languages, everything that can be said. Lyotard says the show was "a reduced monograph of the Library of Babel (that is, of the universe). . . . "[4] Everywhere in its electronic maze were words—heard, seen, projected, and photographed, in neon lights and on computer screens. But the notion that the show, like Borges' story, was about the infinite library is more than a metaphor; it is also the best way to think about the show: to see it as a book and to ask, what sort of book about our postmodern condition was it?

The sixty-one sites of "Les Immatériaux" fell into five sequences; the principal pathways that ran throughout the maze, they were the "chapters" of this book. As one entered the introductory site, called "The Theater of the Nonbody," the sound track played a fragment from Beckett's *The Unnameable*, which narrates the predicament of an "I" who cannot speak yet cannot remain silent. The site, a mirrored vestibule, then opened onto the five paths, each of which was announced by a window display prepared by Beckett's set designer, Jean-Claude Fall.

Essentially, each path was to demonstrate a different kind of artificial extension or replacement of the body (e.g., the way in which scientific instruments exceed the senses in the apprehension of atomic particles). One was also advised in the catalogue that the five paths or chapters had two sorts of linguistic structure, corresponding, on the one hand, to aspects of communication (from where, to where, how, by means of what, and concerning what messages are sent) and, on the other, to five keywords with the prefix *mat-* (matter, material, maternal, and so forth); these abstract rubrics governed the allocation of sites along the pathways. Thus, all the disparate immaterial things in the show were classified at the start within a *table des matières* (table of contents), and they all concluded in a site called "The Labyrinth of Language"— a world of word-processing, of language stored, analyzed, composed, recomposed, and otherwise manipulated by electronic devices. In the world of "Les Immatériaux," everything starts in the body and ends in language.

Ambulating through the maze became a form of reading. At different points along the way the postmodern reader-*flâneur* passed computer consoles with handy didactic summaries of the sites and, as he entered and exited, a computerized index of the concepts of the show; there was also a bibliography of related readings in the form of a little bookstore. Thus the show, itself a monograph of Babel, led to other books. Apparently, the book—its linguistic order—survives in the electronic world, but altered in its form so that it may simulate this world even as it diagnoses it.

According to Lyotard, language theory not only survives the electronic revolution, but also provides it with its order. "In essence," he explains, "the new technologies concern language" (primarily the language of artificial intelligence). Further, as language determines our "whole social bond *(lien social),"*[5] the new technologies also concern our "being-together." This reasoning provided the show with its project: to illuminate how the electronic world is rooted in language, and how we are bound to one another within it.

And yet how seriously are we to take Lyotard's suggestion that this world can be analyzed through the etymology of the root *mat-* in French words (which has no single function and for which there exists no exact English equivalent), or in terms of structuralist theory about the parameters through which messages can be sent? Are not such linguistic categorizations in reality less a deep hermeneutical fact about our being-together in language than a piece of modernist writing in the manner of Brisset, Borges, or Roussel?

The trope of the Library is hardly new or postmodern; in the '60s Foucault saw it as a central metaphor of the modernity initiated by Flaubert and Manet:

> Flaubert is to the library what Manet is to the museum. They both produce works in a self-conscious relationship to earlier paintings or texts . . . [They] are responsible for books and paintings within works of art.[6]

It is through the metaphor of the Library that "Les Immatériaux" managed to infuse the electronic world with modernist meaning. Thus we arrive at the fabulous premise of this demonstration, with its foreground of electronic gadgetry and its background of modernist textuality: that the "book" on or of our postmodern electronic condition is in fact a modernist one!

Baudelaire announced "modernity" within a still Romantic vocabulary; here Lyotard announces "postmodernity" in a modernist idiom. "Thus he goes, he runs, he searches . . . what is he seeking? . . . something we might call *modernity*," said Baudelaire, 122 years ago, of the Painter of Modern Life. Now we have the philosopher

Lyotard running in search of what we might call postmodernity "for no better word is at hand to express the idea in question."[7] There is still the modernist quest, the uncertainty, the confrontation with the "unnameable." But now, like the worried jogger with his Walkman, the postmodern *flâneur* carries with him the tape of modernist textuality. It comes to him in defamiliarized form like the voice of a bygone era, like the beautiful relics of modernist "nontheater" which are the signposts of his quest. Thus, for all its immaterial electronics, over the entire show hung the shadow of what in his analysis of Pop, Barthes called "this old thing called art."[8]

MELANCHOLY AND MANIA

For Lyotard, "Les Immatériaux" was involved in "a kind of grieving or a melancholy with respect to the ideas of the modern era, a sense of disarray."[9] And in the show (or at least in its conception), a sort of oscillation between melancholy and mania replaced high-modernist anxiety. For the art melancholic, nothing seems intellectually at stake in "advanced art" any more, and theory becomes a space of mourning for this loss. (Lyotard finds this melancholy in the "negative," "almost cynical" approach of Theodor Adorno, "which is the measure of the breadth of his despair.")[10]

"Mania" meanwhile is the opposite reaction to this lost object of art: a plunge into the mad, groundless reproduction of things. In *this* state one gets the sort of hysteria of electronic culture which Paul Virilio calls "speed," a catastrophic panic before an endlessly future-shocking condition;[11] one also gets the consumerist thrills or "intensities" which Fredric Jameson describes as "free-floating and impersonal . . . dominated by a curious form of euphoria."[12] Along with its "latent or implicit . . . melancholy,"[13] "Les Immatériaux" manifested this mania in its frantic multiplication of images and in its mad electronic exuberance—its jumble of installations and profusion of computers. "Les Immatériaux" was itself manic-depressive.

Jameson is impressed by the "waning of affect" in postmodern culture—the affect of high-modernist anxiety or alienation. Such angst has its formal apotheosis in absolute abstraction: white monochromes, the blank page, the hours-long fixed camera, in which representation is pushed to its limits—extinction. Anxiety is the affect associated with the end of representation: the heroic encounter of the artist with the strange object that dispossesses him or divides him from himself. Now the end of representation has become a general feature of our world or condition, of the endless recomposition of things; it is not only a matter of art. So, instead of anxiety, we have melancholy and mania, tropes of a postmodern condition, "subjectivity" in a culture which can no longer place the human subject at its center. We also have one sense of "immateriality": in formalist modernism, the end of representation assumed the form of a purification of the basic "materials" of art. Now the criterion of the specificity of medium or material can no longer be used to separate "art" from the decadent "kitsch" culture it was meant to save us from. The great question of modernism was: what is art? Now it is replaced by the postmodern question: who are we in all of this?

DISLOCATIONS

In his writings Lyotard's answer to this question starts with "technoscience." Technoscience transforms the State and economic production; it alters the nature of knowledge; it redefines the very ideas of "art" and "culture." Philosophically, it causes the questions "What is Enlightenment?" and "What is Revolution?" to be replaced with the questions "What is technoscience?" and "Who are we in it?" The postmodern condition is a technoscientific one.

One difference between the industrial revolution and the electronic one is the central place of abstract science in it: to build a steam engine no advanced physics is required. The interlocking of science and technology, today symbolized by Silicon Valley, is of recent origin. But as science and technology become a single thing, it becomes increasingly implausible to think of them in terms of the progressive, optimistic values of the Enlightenment: the I. G. Farben chemical complex ends in the death camps. Thus, Lyotard thinks that what is at issue in technoscience is not the enlightened values it might embody, or the consensus about the nature of the physical world it might make possible, but its singular new place in society, and the deadly reach of its consequences.[14]

These controversial views of Lyotard supplied the philosophical framework for the notion of "immateriality" which gave the show its title. To understand this conception and its connection with our postmodern condition, it is useful to distinguish two sorts of technoscientific "immateriality."

First, there is the electronic dispossession of the human body. "Les Immatériaux" was a phenomenologist's nightmare; everywhere one was shown the replacement of the material activities of the "lived body" with artificial ones, or with formal or immaterial languages. One entered a world of simulation of the body: eating and sleeping (represented by a fast-food display and the Japanese sleeping cell), but also thinking and seeing (the computers and scientific instruments). There were filmic and video simulations of movements and memories, and even a display in which "human" skin was fabricated.

In short, the show suggested that life and death are subject to technoscientific intervention and redefinition. For example, in the site "Vain Nakedness," photographs of Muybridge's 1887 *Animal Locomotion* were juxtaposed with stills from Joseph Losey's film *Monsieur Klein* of anatomical dissection in the Nazi death camps. And in the site "Angel," different photomontages displayed the possibilities of transsexualism and hermaphroditism, while on the sound track a feminine voice (that of Dolores Rogozinski, who arranged all the writings) mused on mythologies of sexual difference. Apparently, even gender succumbs to technoscientific manipulation, as transsexual operations open up the specter of a "third sex." Finally, in the site "The Small Invisibles," it was demonstrated that bodily senses no longer supply the empirical court of appeal for scientific theories. Today, space and time, once thought to be the "forms of intuition" of the world that the body experiences and science studies, exist largely as complex theoretical constructs from which is created the artificial world in which we live.

Second, there is the dematerialization of space. It is not just that we no longer build solely from the materials of our earth. (One site, "Forgotten Soil," presented fragments of brick, wood, and ceramic from buildings of Frank Lloyd Wright and Alvar Aalto as if they were ruins of a lost age.) It is not just that we have elevated the architectural representation to an importance all but equal to that of the building itself. (In the site "Plane Architecture," one was shown how pictorial and architectural codes seem to coalesce in certain works of Malevich and Piet Zwart and, in "Inverted Reference," how the architectural models of Peter Eisenman are so abstract as to become autonomous works.) The sort of civilization technoscience brings with it is endlessly transportable; it goes anywhere. It does not collect people into urban centers; it spreads them out into an atopic anywhere from which they are connected to everywhere by cable: from one's Japanese sleeping cell one tunes into the world. The key image of our immaterial civilization is not the industrial or Saint-Simonian city, but the placeless shopping-center complex.[15]

"Les Immatériaux" simulated our "immaterial" anywhere. The show was not a center around which (industrial) objects were arrayed, but an "implosion" of (postindustrial) things from all over. In this sense, one might say that "Les Immatériaux" is to electronic civilization what the great nineteenth-century universal expositions were to industrial civilization. But this immaterial culture of technoscience was not presented in horrified fascination (à la the humanist vision of a dystopian technology). The aim of the show was not ideological critique, and Lyotard has no use for the category of "alienation" (it is a piece of outmoded theology, he says).[16] Contemporary dislocations of body and place, or the impossibility today of continuous narrative, are not simply the evils of commodification or kitsch; again, these postmodern conditions are already announced in the modernist texts of Beckett.

Technoscience, then, should not provoke a Romantic nightmare. Lyotard wants us to think of it instead as a modernist text in which we can continue the war of heterogeneous invention—once the province of advanced art—by other means. The danger he sees in technoscience is not an alienation of our supposedly natural identity; it is the "totalitarian" possibility that there exists only *one* artificial identity; it is the "totalitarian" possibility that there exists only *one* artificial identity that submits us to centralized control. It is the danger of a homogeneous unity of languages reflected in the informationalist vision of controlled communication. The question "Who are we in all of this?" need not have a single answer; "we" are not a single entity which technoscience alienates or realizes. Rather, in inventing new heterogeneous languages, we constantly reinvent ourselves—that is what modernism has to tell us about our postmodern condition. Thus, Lyotard's "map" is not intended to provide a path out of the postmodern condition, but to accelerate and complicate incommensurable diversity from within, to insure that technoscience be a "heterotopia" of the babbling of languages rather than a utopia of a single world for a single people.

THE AMERICAN VIDEO GAME

"Postmodern" is a label coined in America. It refers, says Lyotard, to "a subject the French don't know very well, since they're always turned so completely in upon themselves."[17] And yet, in America, following Hal Foster's useful distinction, we already distinguish between two forms of "postmodernism," one of which is French-inspired or poststructuralist.[18]

There is a curious aspect of the current debate over postmodernism. It is the confrontation of the advanced French thought of the last twenty years with American mass culture. (One saw this in the audiovisual juxtapositions of the show: a text by Artaud near an image of Elvis Costello, etc. Indeed, an American, making his way through the sixty-one sites, listening in his headset to the ponderous intonation of such "fast" metaphysics as "the world is a video game," might have had a wearied impression of déjà vu.) Jameson thinks that at bottom postmodernism is the name of the strange sort of culture America spreads throughout the globe and into the heavens: "this whole global, yet American, postmodern culture" is carried forth by a "whole new wave of American military and economic domination throughout the world."[19] According to Jameson, the ironies of international capital would have it that the great flourishing of modernist writing and theory in Paris, in which the self-centered linguistic text was cut free from all moorings in the world, finds its sorry realization in the delirious theater of commodities and signs that is the contemporary American shopping mall.

Perhaps never since Adorno blamed the Enlightenment for Los Angeles has there been such a monumental effort to find a place for "Americanism" in the history and philosophy of Europe as in the postmodern debate. Indeed, Lyotard, referring to Virilio's vision of the "overexposed" city, remarks that "Les Immatériaux" is a miniature simulation of what it is like for a French intellectual to travel somewhere between San Diego and L.A. with nothing but his car radio to mark the changes.[20]

The period of high modernism was a period of the "American in Paris," of the cosmopolitan pilgrimage to the "capital of the nineteenth century." In America, where a diasporic modernism was once greeted as a preservation of the "value" of art in the face of the decadence of "kitsch," modernism became the official ideology of a new wave of museological proliferation. Now it is Paris which looks into a future dominated by American-Japanese electronic culture, and attempts to put that culture into *its* museum.

The entrance of advanced French theory into the museum comes at a time in which, in an international philosophical debate, that theory is under attack as "irrationalist" or "relativist." For such opponents the extravagant dilemmas the show dramatized will no doubt seem less a diagnosis of our condition than a predictable product of a misguided philosophy. In its broad terms the international debate over "French Theory" has assumed the form of a debate over the reevaluation of the European Enlightenment in a non-Eurocentric age.[21] It is no wonder that America has a capital place in this debate; we have invented the great "postcolonial" kind of "modernization" or "Westernization" seen in Japan.

The great irruption of a cosmopolitan artistic modernism in pre-Stalinist Russia and prewar Europe, with its fitful manifestoes and radical proclamations, has become an ambiguous piece of cultural heritage, both in the Soviet Union and in the West, at least since the cold war set in. And yet, between here and there, modernism may survive in "French Theory," with all its claims to radicality and celebrations of heterogeneity. This survival of modernism in the very thought on and of our postmodern condition was the final, perhaps unintended, implication of "Les Immatériaux."

NOTES

1. Quoted in French *Vogue*, June–July 1985, p. 476.
2. "A Conversation with Jean-François Lyotard," *Flash Art*, March 1985, p. 35.
3. Jean Baudrillard, *Simulacres et simulation* (Paris: Galilée, 1981), pp. 93 and 99.
4. Quoted in *Le Monde*, May 3, 1985.
5. Jean-François Lyotard, *Tombeau de l'intellectuel et autres papiers* (Paris: Galilée, 1984) pp. 48 and 83.
6. Michel Foucault, "Fantasia of the Library," in *Language, Counter-Memory, Practice*, trans. Donald F. Bouchard and Sherry Simon (Ithaca; Cornell University Press, 1977) pp. 92–93. For Foucault, the metaphor of the Library represents the break between the classical art of rhetoric and the modernist writing of a "heterogeneity of languages," a heterogeneity which insures that there can be no fixed vocabulary or master discourse. This condition, which Lyotard elsewhere terms postmodern, may thus have a modernist basis.
7. Charles Baudelaire, *Oeuvres complètes* (Paris: Gallimard, 1961), p. 1163.
8. Roland Barthes, *L'Obvie et l'obtus*, (Paris: Seuil, 1982), pp. 189.
9. "A Conversation," p. 33.
10. Ibid.
11. Paul Virilio, *L'Espace critique*, (Paris: Bourgois, 1984).

12. Fredric Jameson, "Postmodernism, or the Cultural Logic of Late Capitalism," *New Left Review* (July–August 1984), 146:58.

13. "A Conversation," p. 33.

14. The "new science" of the seventeenth and eighteenth centuries grew up within the ideology of the Enlightenment; but this ideology is no longer required to support it. It can be transplanted anywhere; it is compatible with many different sorts of political regimes; it is used by philanthropist and terrorist, democratic consumer and religious fanatic alike. Its universality lies not in its principles of discussion but in the scope of its technical consequences and in the sort of culture it brings about. Far from carrying enlightened ideas with it, it seems to work without a single ideology or legitimizing narrative. It brings rather the crisis of ideologies in its wake. The war of industrial ideologies is replaced by the wars of postindustrial technosciences.

15. The show was not at all an endorsement of what is known as "postmodern" architecture. Postmodern "historicism" is rather a symptom of a loss of public monumental history in a culture dominated by instantaneous transmission; it is a way of avoiding what Virilio calls "the 'transhistorical' temporality that issues from the technological ecosystems" (*L'Espace Critique*, p. 14). Historicist allusion in postmodern architecture is not simply a stylistic departure from the austerities of the International Style; it may also be a reaction to the "immaterialization of place" that technoscience injects into our world.

16. Lyotard, *Tombeau de l'intellectuel*, pp. 83–84.

17. "A Conversation," p. 33.

18. Hal Foster, "(Post)Modern Polemics," *New German Critique* (Fall 1984), no. 33.

19. Jameson, "Postmodernism," p. 57.

20. Quoted in Lyotard, *Les Immatériaux* (Paris: Album, 1985), p. 19.

21. "Postmodernism" has become the rubric for a philosophical debate about French theory. For example, Jürgen Habermas defends a Weberian conception of modernity and sees in French theory its irrationalist denial. Lyotard challenges Habermas' obsession with "communication" and "consensus" with the values of the incommensurability or heterogeneity of languages. And, while Richard Rorty sides with Lyotard against Habermas' foundationalism, he nevertheless finds in (American) pragmatism a way of maintaining solidarity with enlightened modernity.

SIX

Postmodernism in a Nominalist Frame

THE CATEGORY

In a little more than a decade, postmodernism has grown from a tentative and disputed critical category in a few obscure journals of architecture and dance into a field of academic specialization, such as the Renaissance. It has created sales, and carved a theoretical niche for itself in publishing. It has become the topic of a seemingly endless series of symposia and anthologies competing with one another for being international and interdisciplinary. It has acquired wide journalistic self-evidence. Thus it has become a rather familiar discourse. And yet it is not dominated by a single theory or theoretician. It does not comprise a School of Thought. And, increasingly, those who helped to introduce the category are becoming disagreeably surprised by its fate.

The success of the category does not derive from its coherence. On the contrary, it is used to refer to a motley and elastic range of things. The specificity of the category may be found, rather, in its history: in the way it started, evolved, and took hold in so many

This essay first appeared in *Flash Art International* (November–December 1987), no. 137 (Milan).

cultural institutions. Thus the study of the category may be more revealing than the study of the thing. It may be studied in the manner of what I have called (in reference to Foucault) "historical nominalism." One would inquire through what historical processes postmodernism as a category has managed to so populate our cultural world as to appear as its dominant one.

DATING THE CATEGORY

A good date for the terminological emergence of postmodernism in its present shape is 1975–76. Of course, it had been used for various and sundry purposes long prior to that moment. But those uses had never given rise to the hybrid field of social theory, literary criticism, cultural studies, and philosophy that helped turn the term into a self-evident journalistic label.

In 1975 the rejection of Mies van der Rohe and the international style attracted media attention. It was the year a few eyebrows were raised over Tom Wolfe's racy pop exposure of theoretical chic in American art. It was the year when David Salle and Eric Fischl came to New York seeking fame and fortune. In 1976 *October* was launched, a journal which was to exert a key influence in introducing new theoretical perspectives into the discussion of art in America. From several quarters then there was dissatisfaction with the category of modernism in the arts, and a desire to go beyond. Modernism appeared as a normative restrictive concept from which one sought release. A good date for the take-off of the category of postmodernism that would supersede it is 1979–80. At that time Fredric Jameson gave a larger meaning to the term, as did Jean-François Lyotard, who brought Jürgen Habermas, and eventually Richard Rorty, into the debate. Postmodernism started to become the name of conflicting social theories and philosophies, and the category began its migrations into many fields and countries.

CONCEPTUAL MIGRATIONS

A) The central theoretical influence on American postmodern discourse is the Parisian philosophical and intellectual discussions of the last twenty years. Yet Foucault rejected the category; Guattari despises it; Derrida has no use for it; Lacan and Barthes did not live, and Althusser was in no state, to learn about it; and Lyotard found it in America. It is used, nevertheless, to refer to the thought of such French authors taken as a group. As such it represents a process of homogenization, a reduction of what was once original and diverse work to a few common slogans. Its acceptance is also a sign that Paris no longer controls the designation of its own thought. Postmodernism is what the French learned Americans were calling what they were thinking.

B) The category went into social theory where it is sometimes said to refer to a new stage in capitalism or to the art of the post-industrial age. It was in social theory that the category underwent one of its most startling transformations. The very idea of "modern" it was supposed to come after was changed. At first there was the idea of modern art, a movement with schools and trends that began in mid-nineteenth century Europe and was continued in the postwar New York art; postmodern was to come after it. Then this idea of modern was confused with another—the philosophico-sociological idea. Philosophers often make modernity in their discipline start with Descartes and the rise of modern science. This was combined with the more general idea of the Enlightenment. Hegel said a modern society was the one whose values were distinguished according to the topics of Kant's *Critiques:* science, morals, and art. Heidegger said modernity was instead subject-object thinking. Philosophically minded sociologists eventually came to speak of modern as distinct from traditional societies.

This sort of modernity has little to do with that of modern art. It is not what Baudelaire meant when he used the term *modernité.* Modern art starts with Baudelaire or Manet, not Descartes or Kant, in the nineteenth and not the seventeenth century. It refers to the modernity of Schoenberg's music, so influential for Adorno, and not the modernity Adorno thought Schoenberg might be dialectically negating. Adorno was important for the passage of one meaning of modernity to the other. It was in reference to his thought that the curious view emerged that postmodernism consists in a one-sided or undialectical rejection of the enlightened values of science and democracy.

C) The category also migrated in another direction; it went into what, in America, is called literary theory. It was primarily in literature departments that the French thought of the last twenty years was read and assimilated. The philosophical puzzlement over writing created a new space of academic discussion in these departments which other disciplines at first refused but later envied. The background was American "new criticism," and the central influence was Derrida. Indeed, as a ubiquitous buzzword, decon-

struction may be said to precede postmodernism; the word prefi-
gures many of the patterns of passage into common usage shown
by postmodernism; and, of course, postmodernism is sometimes
said to *be* the art of deconstruction. In architectural discussion, we
already find talk of deconstruction as an architectural practice.

In literary theory, there had already been one use of the term
postmodern. It referred to a literature about itself (as in the *nou-
veau roman*), which was thought to follow upon a period of high
modernism. In the French sources used to make the distinction,
however, the category did not occur. On the contrary, Barthes, for
example, used the term *modernité* to refer to the same literature by
which he meant a single movement that started in the nineteenth
century with Flaubert.

The migration of the category from the New York art world into
literary theory did not resolve this terminological confusion. It had
another effect. The literature professor began to think of himself as
a cultural critic. The privilege of literature or writing as a theoretical object began to wane. Professors of literature began to interest
themselves in video, film, television, or everyday life; greater attention was paid to what in Britain had been called cultural studies.
The key figure in this migration of the category is Fredric Jameson:
a literature professor who does Marxist social theory and writes
about art shown in New York.

D) Eventually the literary and sociological meanings of the terms
were combined. Then it was said that poststructuralism (another
name in America for French-influenced literary theory) is the philosophical expression of postmodernism that despises the enlightened values of science and democracy. This synthesis is particularly popular among the followers of Habermas, both in America
and abroad.

E) Lyotard found the term in America. He used it to sum up the
condition of philosophy for the University Council of the government of Quebec. When he found it, of course, he came across something with which he was already familiar, since the category in the
United States was already embued with French philosophy. Lyotard was central in bringing the term back to France; he was also
important in bringing Habermas into the debate. From the European discussions, the category traveled back to America. Eventually there emerged a rather acrimonious debate over who owns the
concept: German sociology, French philosophy, or American pragmatism (Richard Rorty).

F) In Fredric Jameson's work, there had been two apparently

121

conflicting interests. On the one hand, he had an allegiance to a Lukačsian or Blochian conception of artistic work as expressive of the contradictions of a society as a whole, or as the hope of a total community. On the other hand, he had an interest in French textualist theory, and in the subversive place a society would accord to a writing conceived as a linguistic structure analyzable only from itself. Jameson admired both Sartre and Barthes. In the category of postmodernism, he found a way to resolve the opposition between the two interests. He decided that French textual theory was itself expressive, in the Lukačsian sense, of a new kind of culture Lukačs had only started to contend with, a yet more advanced stage in capitalism, a stage associated with America. Thus he took French theory as reflective, in the old Germanic manner, of the emergence of postwar American culture—a culture of multinational finance and mass-mediated electronic gadgetry, that had transformed the globe and so created a new space that had to be mapped.

Writing from California, Jameson depicted us as groping about in a vast labyrinthine edifice for which he was seeking to provide a map. For whom and for what purpose was this map drawn? And when, in his travels, the postmodern cartographer encountered art works or cultural artefacts, were they, as in the good old days, little microcosms or allegories of the whole edifice, or were they rather critical events that showed the cracks or absences in the edifice, and so the contingency of its structure? Or were they yet something else? In Jameson's mapping of the postmodern, there is some vacillation on these questions. Thus he sometimes writes as though there were a new postmodern kind of work. Jean-Jacques Beinex's *Diva*, he proclaimed, was the first postmodern movie. But, on the other hand, he writes as though the works themselves were losing their critical force and becoming increasingly fleeting or transitory occasions for a rapidly consumed intense feeling or mood, to be contrasted with the older modernist feelings of angst and alienation. Jameson started to look for critical work outside the postmodern edifice altogether, in the third world, a place he thought must be unspoiled by our first world modernisms, in which the international capital would find its other, in which therefore the critical work of the future would be coming.

But Jameson's search for new critical work to embody his historical hopes was at odds with the meaning the term postmodern had meanwhile acquired in actual artistic practice: that of a style with an ideology.

STYLE AND IDEOLOGY

The history of avant-gardes has made familiar—perhaps all-too-familiar—the sort of discourse in which art, theory, and ideology all go together. The American conception of modernism had distinguished and opposed two of them: dadaism and formalism. Dadaism is nominalist. It says that the category of art itself is not real, but historically constructed; and it shows this by making artefacts that question what one is willing to count as art. Formalism is, by contrast, essentialist. It says that art, in abstracting from extrinsic content, discovers what it essentially is when left to itself, or when it has only itself, or its characteristic languages, as its object. This is shown in the process through which the arts strip themselves of all but their constituent or minimal elements. Both sorts of art relations claimed to challenge the bourgeoisie, although that claim is now reserved primarily for the Dadaist, or what, following Bürger, is sometimes called the "institutional" avant-garde. Thus the formalist critic Michael Fried could say in 1982 that postmodernism was yet another name for the resurgence of the popular Dadaist avant-garde against formalism and the achievement of abstract art. But, in fact, what came to be recognized as the postmodern style in art secreted its own ideology, neither purely formalist or Dadaist. By postmodern style is meant a flat replication and mixing of previous styles. It is presented as the negation of the formalist view according to which modernism consists in the purification of the mediums of art to their constitutive elements. It says no medium is pure. It is the art that demonstrated this proposition—the art of the impurity of the arts, of the mixing of media, the art of *bricolage*, of throwing disparate things together. It asserts that there can no longer be the isolated work of originality or genius that extends the possibilities of a medium. There can be no such originality; one cannot initiate one's work from oneself.

The demonstration of impurity in an art of appropriation or simulation then advances an ideology. The ideology takes over from modernism or formalism the idea of the increasing reduction of art to its constitutive elements. But it turns this idea around in a nihilistic or apocalyptic proclamation that the process has reached its termination. In reducing themselves to their most primitive elements they would have exhausted all possibility of further innovation: no further advance would be possible. All that would be left is quotation and patchwork offering itself as proof of what Duchamp had already called the death or end of art. Pure art can have

123

no future, but there remains the possibility of an art of the pure simulation of what art once was. Thus art can no longer present itself as an advance notice or hope of a better civilization; but it can illustrate the certainty that such hope is no longer possible, at least in art.

It was Baudrillard who seemed to offer a general theory of this ending of the possibilities of art. It would be part of a more general ending of Reality itself in a kitsch world of endless simulation. His word "simulation" could be adopted for a simple reason. It was a concept through which things could still be *made*. It was something one could show. It was an eminently visualizable idea. It pre-scribed a reproducible technique for making artefacts which sup-pose a general theory no longer of art, to be sure, but of its end. The postmodern style of appropriation and simulation thus presents itself as the alternately depressive or exuberant affirmation that culture is over, or as the defense and illustration of the ubiquity of kitsch.

POSTMODERN THEORY

In the American desire to go beyond modernism, one may thus distinguish two tendencies. First there emerges a style of kitsch quotation supported by an ideology of the end of art, culture, and much else. And second, there emerges a general perplexity before a new American-dominated culture one does not yet know how to map, and whose connection to critical artistic work is in question. On the one hand, there is work without hope. On the other, there is hope without work.

What is astonishing is that on such ideas would be erected a great international theoretical debate. A clue is perhaps to be found in the role of theory itself in this debate. One model of critical theory in art is that of attempting to formulate or resolve the questions thrown up by the art of one's time. Postmodern theory, taken as a whole, does not seem to follow this model.

A typical feature of postmodernist writing in America is to sub-stantiate every idea by reference to some (still preferably Euro-pean) authority, with little or no attention to coherence among them. The validation of the ideas of theoretical authorities is not central to their postmodern use. Rather, theory becomes an arena of authority which comprises a number of diverse vocabularies that can be brought to bear in describing events or trends.

In this respect postmodern theory resembles the anti-epistemological philosophy Richard Rorty calls pragmatism. He thinks philosophy should not be the internal development of ideas, but a "conversation" among incommensurable vocabularies: the use of whatever theories that suit one's purposes, without regard for tradition or consistency. Rorty finds this pragmatic attitude open and pluralistic, and therefore American. Rorty is a postmodern American philosophical nationalist.

But this is not the only way to see the place of America in the postmodern uses of theory. Postmodern theory exemplifies what it is about. The postmodern theorist appropriates ideas as the postmodern artist appropriates styles. Stripped from their original context, these ideas become transportable; they migrate; they are thrown together at will. Postmodernism is theoretical cannibalism; it is the supermarket approach to ideas. One jumbles together the different theoretical idioms available without commensurating them into a single coherent language.

Thus postmodern theory tends to become global. American in origin, the category of the postmodern has an intertheoretical, international elasticity which has never lost contact with the promotion of cultural products; as such it has migrated back and forth across much of the globe. It may thus be said to be a category of a world market of ideas. It is like the Toyota of thought: produced and assembled in several different places and then sold everywhere. For American modernism, Europe was still a central reference. It was the name of the site of an autonomous, cosmopolitan art and culture. Since at least de Tocqueville, in both Americas and Europe, the opposition between pure art and mass culture has regularly been identified with the opposition between American and European culture. This idea is revived in Baudrillard's account of his travels in America.

Postmodernism is a sign of the loss of the colonial model of a universal culture spread out to educate the world at large. It is rather theory for a post-colonial world of products made and sold in different places without a center. It is like the *lingua franca* of this world: it can be made and consumed everywhere and nowhere.

Part IV

ART AND ARCHITECTURE

SEVEN
Duchamp's Joke

THE TWO ABANDONMENTS

Pictorial Nominalism is the first book of a young Belgian philosopher, critic, and historian of art, Thierry de Duve. It marks the emergence of a fresh critical intelligence, and it can be read in several ways. It offers a new, detailed, and extensive reexamination of the oeuvre of Marcel Duchamp. It advances a general view about how the basic categories of pictorial practice—of its objects, its materials, its ways of making things, its forms of subjectivity—are constituted and change, a general view which points to a new aesthetic. It also participates in a project of current interest: the use of elements of "poststructuralist" thought in a revised history of modernism. Among contemporary French-language art historians or critics, de Duve is perhaps the one to take most seriously to task the work of Clement Greenberg, which has been so influential in American discussions of modernist painting. Indeed the book might be read as an elaborate response to Greenberg.

The ambitions and the art-historical novelties of the book make

This essay originally appeared as the Foreword to Thierry de Duve's *Pictorial Nominalism* (Minneapolis: University of Minnesota Press).

it a conceptually and methodologically complex one. And yet, at first glance, it is quite straightforward. It is the study of a singular event—the event encapsulated by a note Duchamp wrote to himself in October 1912 upon returning to Paris from a somewhat disappointing sojourn in Munich, where he had painted what de Duve takes as a key work in his oeuvre, *The Passage of the Virgin to the Bride*. "Marcel" wrote Duchamp "no more painting, go get a job."

With this event de Duve associates the invention of the first instances of what was soon to be baptized with the English neologism "the readymade," as well as with the notes that would go into the unfinished work, the *Large Glass*, a pictorial object, yet not an easel painting. It is the ready-made for which Duchamp is best known: bicycle wheel, shovel, comb, urinal, those manufactured objects selected, titled, signed, and exhibited by an artist, which have received so many differing retrospective interpretations. Duchamp was asking with these objects whether it was possible to make a work which was yet not a work of art. Since then we have, perhaps not unanimously, and under different descriptions, come to accept, to see, to keep, and to show them as works of art. De Duve proposes a particular reading of this complex acceptance.

The basic analytic concept under which he proposes to place this event of the ready-made is a somewhat unusual one—"the abandonment of painting." His argument is that, despite its physical appearance, the ready-made belongs to the history of painting (and not, for example, of sculpture). The ready-made would be a peculiar picture of a singular moment in which the practice of painting would become "impossible," and would have to be abandoned.

The significance of this view might be seen in contrast to the preeminent place assigned to painting, and to abstract painting in particular, in the conception of modernism of which Greenberg was a great exponent. Greenberg thought modernism would lie in the attempt of the various kinds of art to seek out and show the constituent elements, or the languages, intrinsic to them. In this process, painting, and in particular, abstract painting, would occupy an exemplary place. For if in modernism all the arts try to purify themselves, "pure painting" (i.e., abstraction) would most purely express that process. That is why, according to Greenberg, abstraction would stand for art itself, or art-as-such, and why the pictorial avant-garde would "take the lead" in the culture of modernism.

De Duve observes that Duchamp's invention of the ready-made, regarded as an abandonment of painting, occurs in the same years as the turn to abstraction, or the abandonment of figuration, and he proposes that we now read the two abandonments in relation to each other. He does not see two separate events, or two distinct kinds of avant-garde, as did Greenberg,[1] and later, in another way, Peter Bürger. Rather he takes the two abandonments together as part of a larger event; from this he derives another account of the "birth of abstraction," and so of the very idea of art discovering its intrinsic languages—the idea of modernism.

This other history of abstraction is bound up with the larger ambitions of the book. It is a book written in the late '70's when the category of the postmodern started to inflate the theory and practice of the pictorial arts, a situation de Duve characterizes as one of an "ecclecticism and mannerism" (he does not say "pluralism"), which is a symptom of a "reshuffling of the theoretical cards." Perhaps de Duve's sense of this situation might be put in this way: What in those years we ourselves were abandoning, or what was leaving ourselves abandoned or lost, was not the possibility of painting, of art, of aesthetics, or even of abstraction. Rather we were abandoning a particular *idea* of art, its place in society, its connection to politics, the forms of critical thought and judgment it demands of us—the idea which took abstract painting as the great metaphor of art-as-such. To abandon an idea of art is to open the possibility of another. We must understand the loss of this idea as an event that is happening to us, much as we should now see Duchamp's invention of the ready-made as an event that was happening to painting in this time. Accordingly we must now reexamine the emergence of the ready-made in the history of pictorial practice in such a manner as to retrace its lines of descent into our own "ecclecticism and mannerism," into our own "reshuffling of the theoretical cards, . . . to extract the strategic resonance of that abandonment which Duchamp himself called 'a sort of pictorial nominalism' requires in turn that we abandon the modernist horizon of aesthetic questioning."[2]

It is, I think, the hermeneutic reverberations and interconnections between these two abandonments, Duchamp's and our own, which supplies the tension of de Duve's singular identification with Duchamp. Perhaps at bottom to interpret an oeuvre is to seek to break with the identificatory hold it has over one.

In this reading, I think, one might isolate the production of a basic concept which, though not stated as such, runs throughout the book, and helps to draw together its various strategies of analysis. It is a particular concept of *event*. Duchamp would be an artist of an event, the concept of which might provide us with a new and nominalist aesthetic of judgment. For, as de Duvè uses the term, to "abandon" something is not just to discard it. It is to register the moment of its loss or "impossibility" within a work in such a way as to open up, or call for, another history. The invention of the ready-made would be an event of this sort.

According to de Duve, this kind of event was involved in the series of "abandonments" that punctuate the history of the pictorial avant-garde: the instituted requirement to constantly invent significant pictorial novelties which would retrospectively reinterpret what pictorial practice had been. It would fall to Duchamp to expose the nominalist character of the creation of such pictorial events. In his particular relation to the events of the avant-garde would reside the "temporality peculiar to Duchamp" already to be found in the painting *The Bride* of 1912. This peculiar relation would show why Duchamp never had the "fantasy of the tabula rasa," or the certitude of an origin or a radical beginning, as with the futurists, most constructivists, and certain Dadaists. It would explain why Duchamp was never either a utopian or a distopian.

But de Duve also uses this conception of event in the "biographical" part of his study, and in his contention that "where it is strong aesthetically, where it is fertile historically, the work of art is always of a self-analytic order."[3] For the "truth" of this self-analysis would derive from a response to those events that disrupt one's sense of identity in one's work, and expose the conditions that had made it seem self-evident.

It is thus through a conception of the ready-made as a particular kind of event that de Duve attempts to impose on Duchamp's abandonment of painting both a social-historical and a psychoanalytic interpretation. That abandonment is described historically as a nodal point of symbolic "revelation" of a general crisis in pictorial practice in industrial society; and it is described psychoanalytically as an eroticization of the loss of an object in which we invest ourselves through mourning, mania, or melancholia.

EVENTALIZING THE HISTORY OF MODERNISM

The book is structured by a loose biographical plot leading up to the moment when we see Duchamp's abandonment of painting and invention of the ready-made. It is the story of Duchamp's self-invention as an artist, or rather as what he called an "anartist": his desire to become, and to secure recognition as a painter would come to a point where to be a painter and to abandon painting would paradoxically be thought to require each other.

The episodes in this story are inserted into a short, revised history of the pictorial avant-garde, of which de Duve offers compact new *aperçus*, and a general theory. Duchamp's self-invention as an "anartist" would constantly occupy a "transversal" position with respect to the avant-garde—a sort of erotic-ironic assimilation which betrays what it adopts, and which assumes a coherence after the fact with the invention of the ready-made with which Duchamp was in fact to secure recognition.

The *aperçus* of the avant-garde—short portraits of blocks of conflicting thought and practice—match with the two cities of Duchamp's itinerary (before New York): Paris and Munich. To each city corresponds a particular tradition and a particular conception of the avant-garde itself, of technology and craft, and of color. Together they comprise instances of de Duve's general picture of the avant-garde—what I will call the problematization of pictorial practice through successive and overlapping abandonments. De Duve's strategy is to analyze the moment of Duchamp's abandonment of painting as an event that serves to "reveal" this problematization in a way that "resonates" throughout its history.

De Duve proposes to regard the history of what we have come to call modernist painting as a history through which the self-evidence or the common sense of those categories which had permitted one to identify something as a painting were successively exposed—as though painting were a bride stripped bare. "The abandonment of chiaroscuro by Edouard Manet, of linear perspective by Cézanne, of Euclidian space by the cubists, of figuration by the first abstractionists, down to the figure/ground by how many generations of all-over or monchrome painters"[4] served to question what one took to be a painting. This questioning was institutionalized in the peculiar practice of exhibiting new objects that would constantly raise the question: are they paintings? To the social organization of the avant-garde group with its "frantic production of theories, manifestoes, pedagogical programs and philosophical constructions" corresponded a practice of exhibition open to the public "without jury or prize," which turned the question of what it is to classify a given thing as a painting into a tumultuous social drama. It was through this practice that there emerged the avant-garde conception of the "historicity" of the new painting: of what it means to invent or originate a pictorial novelty, in short, of the pictorial event.

The conception of such events, and of their relation to tradition and academicism, was not, however, of a piece. The two cities of Duchamp's self-invention, Paris and Munich, conceived of avant-garde events in two different ways. In Munich the Parisian conception of a strict line of development leading from Realism to Impressionism to Cézannism to Cubism was broken up. The products of those apparently successive "abandonments" of painting were received and assimilated in a different order, and according to a different model: the "secession model." The Parisian avant-garde had worked on a "refusal-model" where it fell to the Academy to determine the criteria of identification of a painting, and to the avant-garde to refuse them. The great battle of personalities, styles, and ideologies of the institution of refusal carried with it a conception of the pictorial event as a radical or revolutionary break with tradition, eventually inducing the "fantasy of the tabula rasa."

By contrast, the Munich or secession model supposed neither a total or radical break with tradition nor the monolithic character of academicism. In this model the avant-garde assumed the right to say what a painting is, when it judged the academic definition to be too rigid or limiting. The novelties of the avant-garde were not seen as a radical refusal, but as a "secession" that expanded the territory by resituating the place of the old and now merely academic tradition within it.

On de Duve's account, it was in Munich that Duchamp was attempting to work out his own "passage" through cubism, and, in effect, in this passage he adopted a version of the secession model. But what he came to abandon, the event that occurred in his work, was the abandonment of painting itself as a *métier* ("Marcel, no more painting, go get a job"). Thus, the impossibility of continuing to paint assumed the form of an appeal to the "secession" from painting to another idea of art that would resituate what painting had been. Duchamp's abandonment was for de Duve an attempt "to give painting a new meaning by acknowledging what has happened to it," by "relating it to the very conditions that make it objectively useless and subjectively impossible to pursue."[5]

In his account of this "revelation" de Duve reveals his own conception of *sources* of the problematization of pictorial practice characteristic of the avant-garde. Those sources would lie in industrialization, and in the new conceptions of the division of labor, the new materials, the new means of pictorial production and reproduction it carried with it. It was they that would make painting seem "objectively useless."

It is here that the thesis that connects the ready-made to the abandonment of painting acquires historical depth. In introducing mundane industrial objects into the "space" of constant pictorial redefinition invented by the avant-garde, Duchamp would be revealing something about the industrial sources of that space. The ready-made would do this in a number of different ways.

One way to which de Duve devotes some attention concerns that reconceptualization of the division of labor, or of the social categories of making things, involved by the supplanting of craft by mass production. In France, he argues, the "arts and crafts" tradition in the style of William Morris, or of the German *Kunstgewerbe*, was poorly represented. A strong division between *beaux arts* and *métiers* prevailed, which goes back to the division introduced in the *Encyclopédie* between *sciences, arts,* and *métiers.* The scientist, the artist, and the artisan were formed in three separate pedagogical institutions: learning by observation, learning by example, and learning by demonstration. From this institutional segregation derived a series of "common sense" distinctions between art as example and concept and art as technique or procedures of the hand, that later would be "problematized" in the avant-garde discussions of the beauty of technology, or the symbolic unity of form and function.[6]

By contrast, in Germany and Central Europe there flourished a rich tradition of decorative or applied crafts, of *Kunstgewerbe.* From that tradition derived conflicting conceptual tendencies that were to find one resolution in the architectural avant-garde: the Bauhaus attempt to endow the technological work of economic necessity with the older values of disinterested artistic genius. In replacing the artisan, the engineer would adopt the traditional value of the artist. Thus, remarks de Duve, while Gropius declared that "architecture is the finality of all creative activity," he surrounded himself almost exclusively with painters. The functionalist program was a way of resolving this "contradiction"; it invented the figure of the *Gestalter* of a new order and a great pedagogical program to educate the masses to a new sort of "plastic literacy." The difficulty was that the famous unity of form and function remained a symbolic one, and had other results than the ones which this utopian resolution of the crisis of artist and engineer had envisaged.

De Duve retrospectively reads the ready-made as a "revelation" of this crisis. Duchamp connected the beauty of technological or industrial products with the end or abandonment of painting, rather than combining the two in the figure of a functionalist *Gestalter*. For the ready-made was an industrial product endowed with the symbolic value of art in virtue of its mere selection and quite independently of its ergonomic function. What it thus revealed was the historical irresolution, and not the utopian resolution of technique and art, or of form and function. Duchamp was not a utopian; he did not dream of a new plastic order. What he invented was not a new art for the masses, but an art of the advent of the abandonment of pure art (which painting had preeminently been) in the new mass society.

In tracing connections of this sort between industrialization and the problematization of painting, and in presenting the ready-made as a revelation of them, de Duve comes to a central question in the revisionist history of modernism: the place of avant-garde thought in the society in which it occurred.

De Duve presents industrialization as a central and complex source of the conceptual problematizations of pictorial practice: the suspension of its "common sense," and of the "world" constructed around it, in which artist, collectors, critics, etc. could play their parts. And yet the thinking, the inventions, the judgments of the pictorial avant-garde were not simply "determined" by industrialization. De Duve is not an industrial determinist, utopian or distopian, and he is at pains to show that Duchamp was not either. The nostalgia for craft is part of what he wants to analyze and to show Duchamp revealed: a crisis in the very conception of technique, métier, production, in the self-evident categories through which the practice of painting had been carried on.

Thus de Duve holds that it does not just *follow* from industrialization that pictorial practice would assume the dramatic new forms that it did; and it is not the case that industrialization *in fact* led to an end to painting. Industrialization is not related to the inventions of the avant-garde as a "mechanical cause," something one might express by a "covering law."

It was not an "expressive cause," something the occurrence of which would be explained by the way it expressed the disunity of society as a whole. Rather it was the source of a singular and nonrepeatable historical invention, which not only survived the "context" that brought it on, but which helped to retroactively reinterpret what that "context" was. Industrialization introduced into pictorial practice the necessity to invent new concepts or ways of thinking by exposing the old ones as nonessential and limiting. Thus it introduced the practice of what, in a phrase he takes from Duchamp, de Duve calls "a sort of pictorial nominalism."

As de Duve elaborates it, "pictorial nominalism" may be said to be the view that the kind of thing we call a picture or a painting is not given by an essential nature. From this it does not follow that the concept of painting derives from "defining institutions"; that, according to de Duve, would be circular. Rather there emerge at various times and places particular "ideas of art" which make it possible to routinely identify particular things as pictures or paintings. The ideas in turn depend on "procedures" which are "formal and conventional, aesthetic and ideological, linguistic and institutional, economic and political" in nature, and which thus derive from various sources. Together these procedures make for the common sense of pictorial practice; they are what permit it to proceed in an unproblematic manner. But they are also open to "events" which alter them; and de Duve's pictorial nominalism is a historical nominalism. It was just such an event that industrialization introduced into painting. It exposed that what had been taken for granted as essential to the practice of painting was in fact only one way of naming or conceiving of it and its possibilities.

De Duve's thesis is that the ready-made was a sort of nodal point in the abandonment of the common sense of pictorial practice, with its exhibiting institutions and its industrial sources. As such it would be, in one sense of Lyotard's title, a "transformateur Du Champ," something that transformed the "field of possibilities" in which paintings could be made. It would mark the possibility in the history of pictorial practice of another history; it would supply the crucial moment or crossroads, where one is placed in a position where one must invent a new "idea of art," since it is no longer possible to continue with the old one.[7] It would reveal that the fact that painting was " 'not happening,' which avant-garde art accounts for through an active destruction of tradition, is a potential, a supply of future possibility. It means not only 'not happening anymore,' but also 'not happening yet.' "[8]

To study an event of this sort is to attempt to reconstitute the complex procedures that composed it, or the complex "lines of

fracture" it introduced. In this one discovers a tacit historiograph-
ical precept of de Duve's style of analysis. Rather than trying to
historicize the events of pictorial practice by showing how they
were socially necessitated, one would, in reinterpreting them,
seek to open up, or to "eventalize" the ways we have come to conceive of that history. One would not "explain" those events by
showing why they *had* to occur; one would "complexify" them
by tracing a field of "resonance" of what they exposed or revealed. In this manner we would always be in the process of distancing ourselves from those events in which we nevertheless find
the origins of our own thought and practice.

ABSTRACTION

How did our obsession with "flatness" emerge? In de Duve's revised history, it comes from the general crisis, of which the ready-
made was the revelation. Painting was dying as craft or métier; it
was reborn through the invention of an essentializing, self-idealiz-
ing idea: the idea of a pure pictorial language. One would show
that a colored surface could be meaningful in itself. As a painting,
it would distinguish itself from mere decoration and industrial
design through the possession of an artistic "subject matter" in the
absence of any figural or iconographic "content." That in virtue of
which it could have this subject matter was the pictorial language.
The idea of a pure language of color and form is found in all the
early abstractionists, for example, in Mondrian's attempt to establish the universal value of his vertical-horizontal symbolism, or his
triad of primary colors. The idea is already set out in 1911 by
Kandinsky in his book *On the Spiritual in Art.*

In reconstructing Duchamp's relation to the invention of this
idea de Duve makes a number of different points. He argues that
Duchamp's famous retinal/conceptual distinction was not the same
one which was a commonplace of cubism, and which is to be found
in Gleizes and Metzinger. It was not exactly a matter of abandoning a retinal art in favor of a conceptual art, as Joseph Kosuth
would argue against Greenberg in 1969.[9] It was not so much abstract or pure painting that was "retinal"; the *idea* of it was. Abstraction was painting placed under a particular idea of art, which
presupposed what the retina was supposed to grasp. In the invention of the ready-made a other idea was involved: another way of
thinking of the whole field of vision and technique, or the visual

and the technological. In this rethinking de Duve isolates the central question of *color* which had been suppressed in at least the more dogmatic geometrical side of cubism.

Concerning color, Duchamp had different ideas from those of Kandinsky. Kandinsky told of a primordial language of colors and forms; one might select a particular shade from the variety of colors and place it on the canvas in such a manner as to reach directly into the depths of the souls of men. For Kandinsky thought that color was in itself a spiritual, a *geistig* thing, a "strange being" that could burst forth from the brush.

By contrast, Duchamp thought one painted not with *colors* but with *paints*—with those "manufactured objects called paints." The tube of paint *was* a ready-made, he said; thus the act of selecting from paints to make a colored surface was in principle no different from the artistic selection of those other manufactured objects, the ready-mades. For this reason, Duchamp admired Seurat as a colorist: his "pointillism" was like a machine operating by effecting in steps a series of choices from a standardized table of colors rather than through the craft of the hand.

De Duve argues that the contrast between Kandinsky's "spiritual" and Seurat's "mechanical" view of painting with colors derives from two distinct and opposing traditions in thinking about color. Kandinsky's views derive from Goethe and a long tradition kept alive in Germany and Central Europe. Delaunay's turn to abstraction comes from a second and French tradition that goes back to Chevreul's research on simultaneous contrast of 1839, which was to influence Delacroix and later Signac. Cubism reacted against it, but it was revived by Delaunay and Kupka. The distinction between the two traditions shows that differing ideas of color went into the turn to abstraction; and, in particular, it exposes a connection, already explicit in Delaunay, between abstraction and the craft or métier through which paintings are made.[10]

When Duchamp said "I wanted to get away from *la patte* and all that retinal painting," he was therefore supposing that the use of colored paints in making a painting was made possible only through an acceptance of particular ideas on the part of the *métier*. He wanted to question and get away from the acceptance of those ideas. In short, he had a "nominalist" view of color in painting that contrasted with Kandinsky's "essentialist" view of a new pictorial order arising out of its fundamental spirituality. In this respect he "resonated" with the path to abstraction taken by Malevitch and

Mondrian. For there the concern was to attenuate the contribution of craft in making a painting; Malevitch's *Black Square* required no savoir-faire at all.

Along with Russian constructivism, the invention of the ready-made thus reveals another way of conceiving of the abandonment of figuration than the one rooted in the acceptance of the idea of a pure pictorial language. In making that idea the central one, Greenberg overlooked Malevitch, and, of course, reviled Duchamp. For de Duve this is a symptom of a blindness in his general theory. Greenberg tried to ground the "abandonments" through which the craft of painting sought to reinvent itself in the nature of the painting as a physical object; he called on the physical characteristics of the canvas to provide the criterion to distinguish painting from non-painting. But this physicalism is in fact a sort of *reductio ad absurdum;* for the blank canvas *is* a ready-made, and one that can be acquired in any art supply shop. In effect, de Duve proposes to reinterpret what Greenberg called the "reduction of painting to its essential conventions" as the series of abandonments in the craft of painting brought on by industrialization. One importance of Duchamp in this revised history is to help to reveal the nominalist character of the use of color and thus to complexify the history of the paths to abstraction.

ANARTISTIC IDENTITY

It is not exactly Duchamp's "biography" that de Duve studies; it is his self-constitution as an artist. The invention of the ready-made was an event that revealed a sort of impasse in the history of our relations with those things we call "paintings." But it was also an event in Duchamp's own relation to himself in his work. His abandonment of painting left *him* abandoned as a painter. The ready-made would emerge at just the moment when being a painter and abandoning painting would have seemed to require each other. It would thus raise the question of who he was in his work.

To describe the event of this question in his oeuvre, de Duve adopts a fresh nominalist assumption. Instead of starting with received conceptions of the artist such as the Romantic genius or cultural hero, and reading the oeuvre in terms of them, de Duve suspends those conceptions and asks how, historically, there emerge the particular practices that secure the sort of relation an artist can have to himself in his work. It is not therefore that an oeuvre expresses or reflects an artist's life, for the concept "the life of an artist" is not given but constructed. Among other things, an artist's oeuvre is a particular way he provides for himself a "symbolic identity," a socially recognizable self-relation. He must find a particular way of "investing" himself, or "abandoning" himself in his work; and his work is thus a manner of conducting his life. The events in Duchamp's life to which de Duve draws attention, or to which he is drawn—his refusals, his travels, his diplomas, his relations with his artistic family—are accordingly read in terms of the problem of the particular forms of his self-investment in his work as a painter.

De Duve advances a general hypothesis to the effect that "the work of art is self-analytic." This does not mean that a work expresses a truth about the artist understood independently of it and its social determinations. "The self-analytic hypothesis . . . does not totally dismiss the determinations that surround the work of art, but it privileges the creative breakthrough, the 'moment' of significant novelty, in which it locates the function of truth of the work." These moments reveal something about the determinations of the work. "For a large part, the function of truth of an art is to say the real conditions of its exercise."[11] To say "the work of art is self-analytic" is thus to say that it consists in the crises it goes through, that it is punctuated by moments of breakthrough or "revelation," which require that one question one's conception of who one is, or how one has invested oneself in it. It is to say that a work is constituted through those events that arrest the self-evidence of one's identity, and open other possibilities which retroactively reinterpret it.

There is then no "idea of art," no ensemble of procedures that allow for the identification of paintings, which does not specify a particular way of being-a-painter, a more or less tacit way of becoming who one is and may be as a painter. An idea of art carries with it a form of "symbolic identity" that allows one to be recognized as a painter, and by reference to which one imagines or envisages oneself and others. This symbolic identity is a social product of sorts; the concepts through which a person can identify himself in his practice are the same ones that hold together the common sense, the tacit "pact" of the practice.

It is with these assumptions in mind that de Duve analyzes the identity of the avant-garde painter. The abandonments, the questioning, the problematizations of the avant-garde instituted a way of being or becoming a painter. From the crisis in painting there emerged the necessity to become recognized through a practice which at the same time refused or questioned the received categories of recognition. One *had* to constantly place new sorts of objects before a nonspecialized, or nonacademic public. This obligation was not a practical norm; it did not tell one what or how to paint. Rather the invention of the new objects constituted a demand for recognition of oneself as a painter precisely in the absence of agreed criteria as to what painting is. It is this demand placed on a non-academic public in the absence of agreed criteria which would be what Duchamp was referring to when he said that it is the viewers who make the work.

It is in this context that de Duve introduces Lacanian categories. There is the "symbolic" means of self-recognition that confronts one as though a Law. There is the "imaginary order" of those ways of envisaging oneself and others in response to this necessity or demand. And finally there is "the real": what is impossible in this demand or task, the impasse from which it arises and to which it constantly returns, the point of abandonment and event, of breakdown and creative breakthrough.

In employing these categories de Duve does not consider himself to be offering a psychoanalysis of Duchamp's life through his work. He uses the categories to characterize the way Duchamp invested himself in his work, his desire and his demand for symbolic recognition through it, and the events that disrupted that desire and made it seem impossible. The moment of his abandonment of painting marked Duchamp's sense of the historical impasse of the métier in industrial society. But it also required an abandonment of his desire to seek recognition as an avant-garde painter. As such it involved a peculiar sort of eroticization of his relation to his own work. In this manner de Duve comes to the question to which Lacan, in his reading of Freud, formulated in terms of "sublimation": the question of the displacement of one's identity onto who one is in and through one's work. De Duve is interested in Duchamp's "extraordinary and enigmatic concern for painting," as though it were only through painting that Duchamp could respond to the necessity to become who he was. It is that concern which his abandonment disrupted and displaced.

IMPOSSIBLE PROFESSIONS

De Duve starts his book with a meta-discussion about the use of psychoanalytic theory in art history and aesthetics. In his continuing reflections on Duchamp after writing the book, de Duve has much less use for this theory.

Basically, psychoanalysis provides de Duve with a very general analogy which he pursues in various ways throughout his study. He uses it to read the figures of bachelor, bride, and virgin, which recur in Duchamp's titles, without referring to their representative contents, as sexual allegories of Duchamp's relation to himself in his work, his sense of its impossibilities, its ironies, and its eroticisms.

One might read the analogy as establishing a certain "resonance" between psychoanalysis and the pictorial avant-garde. Its dates—and not only its dates—would of course make this possible. With Lacan, one is after all dealing with Picasso's doctor, a man who administered shock treatment to Dora Maar, who frequented surrealist groups and wrote for *Minautaure*. Eluard thought that the woman about whom Lacan wrote his thesis in psychiatry was engaged in *poésie involontaire*. Lacan even alludes to Duchamp in the telling context of the place of psychoanalysis in the events of '68, the year of Duchamp's death.[12]

De Duve refers to the famous inaugural dream of the *Interpretation of Dreams*, the dream of giving an injection to Irma, and to Lacan's reading of it. One sort of "resonance" with Duchamp concerns Freud's desire, as revealed through his interpretation of his own dream (and thus through his self-analysis), to secure recognition for himself as a psychiatrist at the very moment he took the practice of psychiatry to be, in his own phrase, an "impossible profession." One might thus read de Duve's "homology" as a comparison between two impossible professions: psychoanalysis and painting. Freud would have sought to be a sort of "apsychiatrist" as Duchamp an "anartist." Lacan made much of Freud's dictum that psychoanalysis sets an impossible task. And perhaps one might find a sort of structural parallel between the history of avant-garde groups and the history of psychoanalytic ones, following both Lacan and Freud, with their founding-father figures, their patterns of splits and crises surrounding doctrinal disputes, their relentless search for symbolic social and scientific recognition in a society in which, at the same time, they sought to expose the repressed sources of such recognition, indeed of the necessary "discontent" in any human grouping.[13]

In its application to Duchamp, de Duve's homology follows a line of sexuality that runs throughout his work, and the titles he gave to it, and helps to characterize its "transversal" relation to the geometry of cubism and the spirituality of abstraction. Central to this line are the figures of virgin, bride, and bachelor, as well as the later invention of the figure of Rrose Sélavy, famously photographed as Duchamp in drag, with whom Duchamp collaborated (one work declares that it is copyrighted by Rrose). The basic scheme is roughly this: the masculine figures would stand for Duchamp's desire and his demand to be recognized as a painter; the feminine figures for the impossibility of doing so, or of the inaccessibility of the object Painting. In this way, what Lacan called "the impossible" in sexual relations, and the impossibility of painting, are related to each other. The impossibility of making a painting, and investing oneself in it as a painter, would match with the basic impossibility of the sexual relation, in oneself and with others.

De Duve's analogy thus allows him to describe Duchamp's own eroticization of himself in his works in response to the enigmatic object Painting in terms of the general psychoanalytic or Lacanian account of a subject's relation to himself (or his image of himself) in response to the constitutive loss or "abandonment" of the Object of his desire. Painting would figure in Duchamp's work as an object a. Thus the famous theme of the "death of painting" can be read in terms of the no less famous Freudian account of death: the mania, the depression, the bereavement for the loss of the object, and the investment of oneself that follows from the attempt to find it again, and so keep it alive. Duchamp's punning redefinition of genius, of what it is to make or create or originate a work, *l'impossibilité du fer*, would be the mark of this loss, this abandonment, this death in his work, and his relation to it. In this way Duchamp's abandonment of painting is placed under a psychoanalytic description: the fear that something was dying, the hope that it might yet live again. The event of the ready-made would be the moment of the breakdown and breakthrough of this self-abandonment: the moment of revelation and self-analysis.

In short, de Duve's analogy supplies a psychoanalytic vocabulary to characterize the "abandonment" in Duchamp's abandonment of painting, and thus of his "extraordinary and enigmatic concern" for it. It is just this vocabulary that Lacan himself used when he came to explicate the Freudian conception of sublimation.

144

By "sublimation," Freud referred to a diversion of the aims or objects of our basically perverse and partial drives, which, in contrast with the repression constitutive of neurotic symptoms, gains a social acceptance or approbation. The question for Lacan is the enigmatic nature of the social value attributed to such deviated versions of someone's particular partial objects. How is it that a social value could originate from an idiosyncratic perverse, asocial desire? It is a sort of "value" that is independent from, though always connected with, the social institutions of patronage or market: the value objects have for us inasmuch as we are embodied subjects of desire, inasmuch as we are talking sexual beings.

We have a sort of love affair with the things we call art. We "overestimate" them. We take them as peculiar parts of our bodily selves which always seem other than ourselves, as things in which we die and live again, and which occasion in us alternating feelings of dejection and omnipotence. They become objects of envy, despair, and exhilaration, and we treat the tradition with which they confront us as a "symbolic debt," or in terms of an "anxiety of influence." In short we treat them as though they maintained within them that which we have lost. Sublimation, says Lacan, is the elevation of an object to the dignity of *Das Ding*.[14]

Sublimation is then the capacity a work has to sustain within it a relation to those peculiar bodily objects we can never represent to ourselves without losing ourselves. In the case of painting, such, according to Lacan, would be the singular position of the gaze as object a. But Duchamp's *impossibilité du fer*, the acknowledgment of an impossibility of painting that would open the chance of another idea of art, would also belong to this order. As distinct from just giving painting up, Duchamp would have "sublimated" its loss in his work and in his relation to his work. This is what would explain his "extraordinary and enigmatic concern for painting" at the very moment of his invention of the ready-made, the moment of revelation of his abandonment. It is this sublimation of the "death" of painting that would give his work its peculiar *humor*.

DUCHAMP'S LAUGH

In the notes to the *Large Glass*, Duchamp anticipated (anticipated *demanding* of his viewers) that the work would be the occasion of an immense hilarity that might withstand the most serious scrutiny. Abandoning painting was apparently an event fraught with great laughter.

De Duve refers to this hilarity as a kind of irony, even finding a pun on "iron" in *l'impossibilité du fer*. And, in general, there is something faintly comical, if not ironical, in the ingenious ways de Duve devises to extend the humor of *calembour* and wordplay, typical of the period and much to Duchamp's liking, into his own allegorical readings of his works and their titles.

Duchamp's humor might be analyzed in terms of the homology de Duve establishes between sexual and painterly identity, or the way Duchamp maintained in his work the impossibility of work by maintaining in himself the impossibility of sexual identity: it is a humor which says that at bottom sexual identity is just as laughable (and laughable in the same way—just as "ready-made") as artistic identity. Indeed there is something humorous about identity itself. The "constitution of the subject" is inherently comical, since it derives from a fundamental impossibility. Duchamp's humor would be the humor of our attempts to ever remain the same.

It is a sort of humor that requires what Duchamp called "precision"—just the right amount of "vulgarity." It must expose the incongruities in those practices through which identity is secured. In her discussion of Duchampian hilarity, Molly Nesbit draws attention to the early cartoons: in them there already is, in a sexually charged context, the wit of incongruities [15]—or, of what Lyotard calls "incommensurabilities," [16] the incommensurabilities of word and image, the retinal and the conceptual, the artist and the viewer, the commensuration of which would render pictorial practice unproblematic or self-evident. One must hold together these elements of a now "dying" pictorial common sense in a sort of "suspended animation." As such they would constitute a vast art-historical joke.

This *jeu*, this play with the incommensurabilities of painting, this art of divesting one's investment in it, this game with objects, with words, and with oneself, would be a way of putting into play the loss of the possibility of painting, and of opening its practice to other possibilities, other histories. It would be a way of maintaining, or keeping present in one's work, what one is in the process of losing, unlike the "mania" that would deny it, or the "melancholia" that would incorporate it. It would comprise a way of responding to the advent of the abandonment of painting different from the famous heroism of the artist before those "anxious objects" that would be his works. That is why it could serve as an antidote to the great spiritualizing enthusiasm for pure art, with the great exhilaration Kandinsky associated with the capacity of a colored surface to express through correspondence the movements of the soul. What was required was the precision of injecting the right touch of industrial vulgarity into such *geistig* pieties of painting.

In its sublimatory function, this "indispensable vulgarity," this "hilarity" would point to a source of "value" in painting different from, and perhaps prior to, the "values" of quality, taste, and beautiful form of appearance: the value of incommensurability. It is the value in the wit that moves from those "value judgments" that assert "this is beautiful" to those which ask "is this a painting?"—the values of a "sort of pictorial nominalism." Duchamp's hilarity would be a sort of nominalist humor, a laugh at the expense of categorial identity.

A NOMINALIST AESTHETIC

In October of 1912, returning to Paris from Munich, Duchamp thus wrote to himself "Marcel, no more painting, go get a job." De Duve's complex study of this little episode brings us to the point where a problematization of pictorial practice brought on by industrialization gives rise to the eroticized wit of the incongruities of identity. At this point—which is the point of the invention of the ready-made as an event—two general questions are raised and connected to each other: the historical question of "originality," or what it is to originate, create, or invent something, and the psychoanalytic question of "sublimation," or how we invest ourselves as embodied subjects of desire in those works we originate, create, or invent. It is these questions which the hilarity of inserting mundane manufactured objects into the space opened up by the pictorial avant-garde would, at least retrospectively, address to us.

It is these same questions, which, I think, de Duve would introduce into our own "abandonment of the modernist horizon of aesthetic questioning," of which the mannerism, the baroque eclecticism, of our "postmodern condition" would be the symptoms. In an earlier essay de Duve isolates what he takes to be the "central aporia of postmodernism."[17] We have only been able to conceive of what we call the postmodern through the historicist or avant-garde categories of modernism. The more one conceived of it as a radical break or rupture, the more one fell back on the very system of ideas from which it was supposed to break.

But the postmodern need not be conceived as yet another modernist rupture. We may think of it, in a Duchampian manner, as an event we still do not know how to name, but which causes us to rethink and to put into play what has led to it, as distinct from "refusing" the past, or declaring it dead. The postmodern is not an end to pictorial originality, but the arrival of another conception of it. It is the arrival of a new kind of aesthetic questioning.

Perhaps we are in the process of losing the Romantic image of the genius-hero in our conception of what it is to respond to a crisis in our practices, and to invent or originate something new. Abandoning the modernist idea of a pictorial essence would expose our incredible investment of ourselves in the idea of art-as-such. In response to the problematizations of our practices and ourselves in our practices, we are no longer capable of searching for this sort of spirituality. We *can* no longer make the utopian assumption of a purity of expression that would offer the horizon of a new order, either technological or anti-technological. For us, the necessity to originate something—to create or to invent—is not that of a new order that would arise out of the demise of our old one, and in which the ideality of art and the creativity of man would at last coincide with each other.

It is rather those moments of "impossibility" which disrupt our practices, and the ideological and institutional self-evidence through which they proceed, that seem to have come to compel our inventions, to compel them with a necessity which, while it does not prescribe what we should do, cannot be avoided: those moments which offer the "chance" of our inventions. Perhaps the source of our originality has come to lie with those events which expose the history of our practices to other possibilities: the events of the "not" in Duchamp's formula "a work which is not a work of art." In any case, it is in our relation to such events, to what is happening to us no longer and not yet, that we might find a new kind of aesthetic questioning. For this "not" shows that a work is always more than an object combined with an ideality given to the critical capture of a subject. It shows that it is a fragile and contingent unity of disparate elements, in which we come to invest ourselves, and which is brought together for a moment by those materially rooted "ideas" which allow us to classify things by their aesthetic names.

Nominalism is the doctrine that only individual or disparate things exist, and that our classifications of them are only contingent and changeable inventions. Pictorial nominalism is the view that the "ideas" which allow us at a time and place to classify things pictorial are open to problematizing events, and are not fixed by an essential nature. The aesthetic of such nominalism is the aesthetic that opens these ideas to our judgment. It is an aesthetic not of taste or beautiful appearance (or of the anti-aesthetic or the tasteless), but of the invention of new sensibilities, new concepts, new techniques and ideas of technique in response to those incommensurabilities which question our practices, and eventalize our relation to them.

This sort of aesthetic questioning offers a form of critical intelligence to the art historian. The critical art historian would not suppose, or seek to supply, an idea of the true nature of art, its genres and its forms of subjectivity, so as to understand that history, or show what that history reveals. Rather he would look in that history for the way such ideas have been constructed, and the way they have been exposed to other histories by problematizing events. In this manner he would help to formulate what is happening to us in our own situation; he would help to characterize that from which we are in the process of distancing ourselves. And, it is in terms of just this sort of aesthetic questioning that we might understand the obsessive love, the compulsive fascination, with which this new book invests those now even beautiful relics of a moment in the history of our relation to what we call "art," when the very idea of making a painting could be the occasion of an immense hilarity.

NOTES

1. See de Duve, "Counter Avant-Garde," *Art International* (May 1971), 15:16–19. Michael Fried reformuled the thesis of the two avant-gardes in distinguishing "presentness" from a "theatricality," for which he says "postmodernism" is just a new name. See "How Modernism Works: A Response to T. J. Clark," *Critical Inquiry* (September 1982), 9:217–234.

2. Dust jacket of *Le Nominalisme pictural.*

3. De Duve, *Pictorial Nominalism* (Minneapolis: University of Minnesota Press, 1990).

4. *Ibid.*

5. De Duve, "The Readymade and the Tube of Paint," *Artforum*, May 1986.

6. See Molly Nesbit, "The Body in the Line," *Halifax Essays on Duchamp* (Cambridge: MIT Press, forthcoming).

7. See Joel Fineman "The History of the Anecdote," *The New Historicism*, H. Arnam Veeser, ed. (London: Routledge, 1989).

8. De Duve, "The Readymade and the Tube of Paint."

9. De Duve, "Le Monochrome et la tolie vierge," in *Résonances du readymade* (Paris: Chambon, 1989), pp. 193–280.

10. The role of theories of vision in the work of Duchamp is discussed by Rosalind Krauss, in "The Blink of an Eye," in *The States of "Theory,"* David Carroll, ed. (New York: Columbia University Press, 1989). She makes use of Jonathan Crary's study of historical changes in the conception of vision in the scientific literature of the nineteenth century. See *October* (Summer 1988), vol. 45. One may also note that, since Worff and Sapir, color vision has been a central case for contemporary debates about language and cognition. Thus in *Women, Fire and Dangerous Things,* the linguist George Lakoff presents the case that color vision is embodied vision. His collaborator, Mark Johnson, applies this view via Arnheim to Kandinsky; for Johnson the view that colors are spiritual beings becomes the view that colors are the focal points of metaphorical projections of body schemata *(The Body in the Mind).* In this discussion the realm of the "cognitive" takes over from the more "symbolist" tradition to which de Duve refers. A historical nominalist might then inquire how the embodied cognitive subject of vision has come to be conceived and "constructed" in this new science—for example, what the body must be conceived to be, for it to yield regular results in cognitive achievement tests. A differing account of embodied vision (which also has roots in Helmholtz) derives from the psychoanalytic sources Krauss introduces into her reading of Duchamp. Seeing paintings would not be a merely "cognitive" matter. The body would be involved in other more eroticized ways, in terms of the gaze in relation to which one forms one's bodily self-image or ego, and gives oneself to be seen.

11. De Duve, *Pictorial Nominalism.*

12. Lacan, "Impromptu at Vincennes," *October* (Spring 1987), 40:18.

13. In "Spéculer—sur 'Freud,' " *La Carte Postale* (1980), Jacques Derrida also discusses Freud's self-analysis as a sort of event in his work. He connects this event with the "speculative" character of Freud's thought, with its rhythm of interruptions that initiate new starts. Freud's oeuvre, he argues, is "autobiographical" in a sense that requires us to conceive of autobiography altogether differently, *tout autrement:* not as in psychobiography, where the work is reduced to a mere "empirical subjectivity," and not as in formalism, where the question of subjectivity is eliminated altogether in the consideration of the work. The "Freud" of Derrida's title is thus not the empirical person Freud; it is rather Freud's signature, his idiom, his singular performance; and it is to be discovered through a particular sort of reading—the "abyssal" sort, which reapplies to what someone writes the "scene of writing" it. In this manner Derrida tries to interconnect Freud's speculations on the death drive and the nature of those speculations as a kind of questioning that would constantly interrupt his work in its fits and starts. The *autos* in Freud's "auto-analysis" or "auto-

biography" would constantly be tied up in his work with a response to something "altogether other" *(tout autre)* which necessitates a self-questioning. Freud would constitute himself through his speculations only by trying to "deconstitute" himself through them. This process of questioning and thinking would be prior to Freud's own self-conception as the founder or father of a new science, and would indicate something unanalyzed which recurs in the history of the psychoanalytic movement which he thereby founded. In a similar vein, Samuel Weber, in *The Legend of Freud* (Minneapolis: University of Minnesota Press, 1982) tries to reread Freud in a way that might change or "disturb" our institutionalized relation to "Freud." Like de Duve, Weber is also drawn to the Irma dream. In particular he refers to what, in its interpretation, Freud called "the navel of the dream," or "the place where it straddles the unknown." Thus Weber might agree with de Duve that the self-analytic moment says something about the real conditions of the exercise of a work. The navel might be said to mark the speculative place of the event in Freud's conception of his own self-interpretation (it turns out to be the place where the series of feminine figures is involved in the formation of his dream-wish).

14. For Lacan's views on sublimation, see *L'Ethique de la psychanalyse* (Paris: Seuil, 1989), pp. 105–196; and in reference to the "radical principle of the function" of painting, see *The Four Fundamental Concepts* (New York: Norton, 1978), pp. 110–114.

15. Molly Nesbit, "The Body in the Line."

16. Jean-François Lyotard, *Les Transformateurs Duchamp* (Paris: Galilée, 1977).

17. De Duve, "Marthe Wéry: La Peinture de près et de loin," in *Essais Datés* (Paris: La Différence, 1987), pp. 227–230.

EIGHT

What's New in Architecture?

Architecture is about space, the construction of habitable space. But how and what we build depends on when we build; the construction of habitable space has a history. The question of what is new in architecture is the question of the sort of history it has had, and may yet have. Reflection on this question has involved some contemporary philosophers in two traditional topics: space and time. One might extract a general theme. I will call it the theme of "other time, other space"; and I will indicate how the question of what is new in architecture may be formulated in terms of it.

In an interview concerning architecture, Foucault says modern philosophers have paid too much attention to time, not enough to space.[1] Foucault proposes to rethink space (or habitable space) in terms of his histories of the "constitution of the subject," or, to employ a familiar, and more architecturally loaded term, his histories of the ways we *construct* ourselves. A history of space was a part of his attempt to extend the concept of "technology" to include what he called "technologies of the self." "I think it is somewhat arbitrary to try to dissociate the effective practice of freedom of

This essay first appeared in the *Journal of Philosophy and the Visual Arts* (1990), no. 22.

people, the practice of social relations, and the spatial distributions in which they find themselves."[2]

Urban planners, administrators of political territories, and prison wardens are all concerned with such "spatial distributions"; just as the distribution of domestic spaces forms an integral part of the social and political history of the family.

A central idea in this analysis of habitable space was that the spaces we construct for ourselves to inhabit help to construct ourselves, our ways of being, our ethos. How we are housed helps to determine who we are and may be, and one can thus examine through what means, conceptual and physical, and in response to what problems, we have come, so to speak, to inscribe ourselves in architectural stone.

Foucault's study of such spaces of our own self-construction was "genealogical"; it was thus after all related to time. Foucault held there are *events* in the sorts of spatial distributions in which we find ourselves, in the spaces we construct for ourselves to inhabit. We construct ourselves in part in response to events; and such self-constructions are in turn exposed to other events yet to come. In this sense one may speak, in Foucault's historical work, of the spatial problem of "inhabiting a time."

The events with which Foucault was concerned in his histories were of a particular sort—the events of new kinds of thinking, saying, being, doing, or seeing. That "there are events in thought" was for Foucault a "principle of singularity."[3] An event in thought may be said to be singular just when the novelty it introduces cannot be predicted or explained in terms of context and logic alone. Ian Hacking refers to such singular events when he says that the logic neither of induction nor deduction alone can account for the emergence of the styles of scientific reasoning that determine possible domains of true or false discourse—styles like statistical or experimental reasoning.[4] We can never *infer* an event in thought from the context or reasoning from which it arises; it is always the singular arrival of something new which retrospectively transforms its very context, social and intellectual.

But what Foucault thus says of a statement *(énoncé)*—that it is always "an event which neither the language *(langue)* nor the meaning can ever quite exhaust"[5]—may equally be said of building or housing: the spaces we inhabit are always events that cannot ever quite be exhausted by the meanings with which we invest them.

In Foucault's early paper on architecture, "Of Other Spaces,"[6] we might find a name for such events in the spaces we inhabit. Foucault refers to spaces not of utopia but of "heterotopia"—those spaces which appear singularly unclassifiable in our classifications and the meanings we derive from them—like Borges' Chinese encyclopedia.

And, in Foucault's study of space, how we are housed is tied up with the great question of which kinds of classifications are available at a time and a place for us to characterize ourselves. The housing of the mad or the criminal in the asylum or the prison involved the question of how some things came to be classed as madness or crime, while other similar ones were not. Foucault's conjecture was that such architectural classifications arose in response to particular problems, and, more precisely, to *new* problems, when the response did not just follow from the context and could not be given through a logical working out of existing discourse. There arise problems that call for the invention of a *singular* response; they are the "eventalizing" problems in our architectural self-classifications.

Foucault called such moments "problematizations." A problematization is never the simple consequence of the context or the logic of the historical process in which it arises; it is an event that interrupts the self-evidence of its context, historical and conceptual, and obliges it to modify itself. The "other space" of a classificatory heterotopia becomes historical for Foucault when it assumes the force of the "other time" of an event, when it problematizes the history in which it figures, requiring a singular invention of thought.

Foucault's "genealogical" investigations into the invention of those spaces that have served to construct us was thus concerned with problematizing heterotopic events in the histories in which we find ourselves. He tried to start with a kind of break with the self-evidence of our current ways of going about things (and, in particular, of the sorts of spaces we construct for ourselves to inhabit). This break with our own self-constructions would offer us the possibility of a "space" in which to reexamine the history of just how we came to take those particular kinds of self-construction for granted, and to expose us to the invention of new ones. The aim of Foucault's "genealogy," in contrast to a certain totalizing necessitarian strain in social history, was thus to "eventalize" our history, to help articulate something new in what is happening to us.[7]

Foucault tried to show how that "simple idea in architecture," as Bentham called his Panopticon, was a great *invention* in the history of the spatial distributions in which we find ourselves, and therefore in our social relations and the exercise of our freedom. But to retrospectively analyze the "archive" in which this distribution and these relations came to figure was not to show how implacable it had become. It was on the contrary to break with its air of obviousness, the sense that there was no other way to proceed, and so to let us diagnose the possibility or arrival of other spaces, other ways of constructing ourselves. It was to free the history of our own self-constructions for our invention.

INVENTIONS

An invention, Derrida declares in a 1983 essay, must possess "the singular structure of an event."[8] The essay is about how to rethink invention by rethinking event: Patent law, born of industrial technology, has learned to make invention conceptually manageable and thus "calculable"; and such manageability has been prepared by a philosophical "displacement" in the idea of invention that becomes stable "in the seventeenth century, perhaps between Descartes and Leibniz." To "reinvent invention" is to extract its concept from this modern philosophical and legal context by restoring and radicalizing the sense of "surprise" in what it initiates or innovates: the "implicit contract" it must violate, the "disorder" it must introduce into the "peaceful arrangement of things." "Invention" shares roots with "event"; both derive from *venire*. To invent is to "come upon" something for the first time. It thus involves an element of novelty or surprise, which would be of a singular sort when what the invention comes upon could not previously be counted as even possible in the history or context in which it arises. It is then an "invention of the other"; it initiates what could not have been foreseen, and cannot yet be named.

The lecture containing such reflections on the event in invention is one Derrida selects out of chronological order to head off, and to entitle, a thick volume of recent writings; and in a foreword he explains why. He says the lecture was a "pivotal" one in the movement of what he terms his *théorie distraite:* the "dissociated, separated, *distracted*"[9] elements of an assemblage in which would be variously traced something of his "formation" in the '80s. The emergence or the arrival of a disparate multiplicity—that is roughly what Derrida understands as an *event*. And, by its very conception, deconstruction must have this sort of "history"; it must proceed by constant disparate invention. "Deconstruction is inventive or it is nothing . . . its process engages an affirmation. The latter is tied up with the to-come of the event, of the advent, and of the invention."[10] And among the disparate elements of this "mobile multiplicity" in the thought of a rather particular first person in deconstruction, there figure the writings Derrida devoted to "architecture," or wrote in "co-respondence" with his "friends" in architecture, Bernard Tschumi and Peter Eisenman—friendship being defined as a shared responsibility for the affirmation of the event that is presupposed by deconstructive questioning ("If the question *corresponds*, if it corresponds always to some demand coming from the other, then it lets itself already be preceded by a strange affirmation").[11]

In this manner Derrida would have again "come upon" architecture for the first time. He would have been guided by his sense of responsibility (or "co-responsibility") for those events one does not yet know how to name. And he would discharge this responsibility by introducing into architecture the concept of event ingredient in the idea of invention that is to be reinvented. Thus he asks whether "an architecture of the event" would be possible, as though he were asking what an "invention of the other" possessing the "singular structure of an event" would mean for architecture, and for the architectural allegory of thought, and therefore of invention in thought.

More particularly one may distinguish three points in the "invention" Derrida brings to architecture; they might be said to constitute three points in his response to the question what is new in architecture.

1. There exist "events" in our history: those singular occurrences that open up "new" or "altogether other" possibilities in the history in which we find ourselves. As Derrida uses the term, an "event" does not refer to a narrative occurrence (as in what the *Annales* historians castigated as *histoire événementielle*). It refers not so much to what takes place in a narrative or an *histoire* as to those unanticipated turning points which interrupt it, and the world its protagonists inhabit. An event is the unforeseen chance or possibility in a history of another history.

Derrida would recognize such events in the history of sciences and forms of reasoning, or in the question common to a number of different historians of science: "How does one divide up, and how does one name, those conceptual ensembles that make possible and receivable such an invention, when the later must in turn modify the structure of this very context?"[12] But there are also political examples; Derrida calls 1968 "that event one still does not know how to name other than by its date."[13]

To speak of an "architecture of the event" is thus to ascribe to architecture (or to introduce into the conception of an architecture) a peculiar sort of historicity, or relation to history. In terms of the architectural allegory, it may be contrasted with the "monumental,"[14] if by "monument" one understands something built once and for all, with a single origin or end, with a "proper body," of which the Greek metaphysics of formed-matter would be a first philosophical articulation. An architecture of the event would be an architecture of this other relation to history: it would "eventalize" or open up, what in our history, or our tradition, presents itself as "monumental," as what is assumed to be essential and unchangeable, or incapable of a "rewriting," as what is "fixed in concrete." It would, as it were, interrupt or dislocate, what the *demiurgos* or architect of History would be thought to have constructed once and for all in conformity with a given plan, program, or model. It would, says Derrida, *s'explique avec l'événement*, would be explained by, and would give an account of itself in relation to, those events which interrupt or dislocate the world we inhabit, or what we assume to be monumental in it. And this would involve *un mode d'espacement qui donne sa place à l'événement*, a way of spacing that gives its place to the event.

2. Our response to such "events" in our histories requires a questioning of the "value of habitation." The value of habitation is the value of *Heimatlichkeit*, of being brought together in a proper appropriate place or of being able to find ourselves at home in such a place. It is a value strongly represented by Hegel, who said "philosophy is just this: being at home with oneself."[15] Derrida refers thus to the "uninhabitable," what is *unheimlich*, at once strange and familiar in our being together in what we take to be our proper time and place. The uninhabitable is then what exposes or opens up our received ways of inhabiting to events.

Derrida has roughly this general story: for a long and powerful tradition of thought which we still "inhabit," to construct a habitation, a way of living, has meant to construct a space in conformity with a plan, an ideal, a model, essence, or nature, that would be independent of it, of which the well-ordered household, or *oikos*, would stand as a great paternalistic allegory. The task of inhabiting the uninhabitable is to conceive of another relation of our being-together in a space and a time than this one. Derrida's twenty-ninth aphorism says:

> To say that architecture must be withdrawn from the ends one assigns to it, and, in the first place, from the value of habitation, is not to prescribe uninhabitable constructions, but to interest oneself in the genealogy of an ageless contract between architecture and habitation. Is it possible to *faire oeuvre* (to make something, to make a work) without arranging a mode of inhabiting?[16]

To make a work that does not arrange a mode of inhabiting is to provide or maintain in a work a space for the chance of another history. The problem of "inhabiting the uninhabitable" is the problem of how to construct ourselves and live in a world, when we accept that at bottom there is no essence, no plan, no program of our being-together in the spaces we inhabit; that, in those spaces there always exists the possibility of an event that would dislocate what we assume to be natural essential or "monumental" about it.

3. In response to the "surprise" in our received ways of inhabiting things, we must let ourselves be put up for "invention." We cannot say we must invent *ourselves*, for it is just ourselves who are "surprised" by the event; and Derrida refers to a " 'we' that finds *itself* nowhere, that doesn't invent *itself*."[17]

> ... [the event] does not happen to a constituted *we*, to a human subjectivity whose essence would be arrested and which would *then* see itself affected by the history of this thing named architecture. We only appear to ourselves from the point of an experience of spacing already marked by architecture. What happens through architecture constructs and instructs this *we*. The *we finds itself* engaged by architecture before being the subject of it: master and possessor.[18]

One might say that in constructing and instructing us, architecture involves itself in a central question which Derrida puts in his pivotal essay on invention by saying *"we are to be invented."* This may be, in Derrida's idiom, the question of our *freedom*.[19]

POINTS OF FOLLY, LINES OF ACTUALITY

"An architecture of the event," says Derrida, would be an architecture of a peculiar kind of "impossibility." In English as in French, we speak of an event as something which "takes place." And, at one point Derrida offers this definition: an event is that "which gives itself place without ever coming back to it *(se donne lieu sans en revenir)*." The phrase makes an idiomatic allusion to *je n'en reviens pas*, "I can't get over it"; an event is the arrival of something we can't get over, which does not leave us the same.

But the phrase also invokes an element of "impossibility." "Such" Derrida declares, "would be the task, the wager, the care for the impossible: to give dissociation its rights but to set it to work *as such* in a space of re-assembly";[20] and in his essay on invention, Derrida discusses this sort of impossibility. "How can invention *come back* to the same *(revenir* au même)?", he asks rhetorically in advancing his idea of the "invention of the other." "It suffices for this," he responds,

> that the invention be possible and that it invent the possible. Then from its origin ... it envelopes within it a repetition, it deploys only the *dynamics* of what already *found itself there*, the set of possible comprehendables which is manifested as ontological or theological truth, program of a cultural or techno-scientific (civil or military) policy, etc. In inventing the possible from the possible one returns the new (that is: the altogether-other which can also be extremely old) to a set of present possibilities, to the present of the possible, which insures the conditions of its status.[21]

An invention of the other, of "the new" which is the other, is thus never possible. It is *not* possible in just the sense that Derrida speaks of what is *not* habitable, and the question of this "not" is the topic of his paper *Comment ne pas parler.*[22] That paper is about a tradition of such paradoxical or paralogical pronouncements as "to think the unthought," "to say the unsayable," "to see the unseeable," or "to represent the unrepresentable." And one may add that "to inhabit the uninhabitable" belongs to it, starting with the discussion of the *chora* in Plato's *Timeus*. It is a tradition tied up with the "mysticism" of the negative theology Derrida discusses, but would also include the early Wittgenstein as well as the later Heidegger; Derrida finds it as well in Freud's discussion of "negation." In the tradition of this "not" Derrida discerns a notion of necessity connected to the chance or possibility of an event. We cannot avoid betraying that of which we cannot speak (represent, inhabit, etc.); we cannot *but* avoid it; such is the necessity of what is not possible for us.

In the philosophy of Gilles Deleuze we find a distinction that is useful in grasping this idea of the impossible. Deleuze offers a somewhat different account of the sequence in the seventeenth century involving Leibniz. He has Leibniz hesitating between two distinct concepts, the concepts of "the possible" and the concept of "the virtual." (The best of all possible worlds might thus be said to be the one with the greatest *virtuality*). In his somewhat untraditional use of the terms, "possibility" for Deleuze is the concept of something which might exist but does not; it contrasts with "reality," as when one speaks of "realizing" possibilities. It follows that "from the point of view of the concept, there is no difference between the possible and the real";[23] and the reason for this is that the idea of possibility is always taken from that of reality. It is this notion of possibility that is supposed by schemes of theological evolution. It is also supposed by the probabilistic view of evidence, or by induction.[24]

By contrast, for Deleuze, the "virtual" is a reality of which we do not yet possess the concept; and it is not "realized" but "actualized." Actualization is a process of differentiation, but this differentiation cannot, by definition, be given or anticipated by our concepts; it cannot be said to be more or less probable; its description cannot yet be assigned a truth-value. A "virtual multiplicity" is a disparate set of things of which we cannot yet have the concept; and its "actualization" therefore involves the invention of something which, by the lights of our concepts, is impossible. "These lines of differentiation are therefore truly creative; they actualize by inventing."[25] An event for Deleuze is not a history or a drama with beginning and end; it is the creative or inventive actualization of a virtual multiplicity.

The "virtual" thus involves something which is not yet seeable, thinkable, or sayable in what we see think or say. But this negation, says Deleuze, is not a logical one; the virtual is not the obstacle or reversal of the possible: "one has only to replace the actual terms in the movement that produces them to bring them back to the virtuality actualized in them in order to see that differentiation is never a negation, but a creation, and that difference is never negative but essentially positive and creative."[26]

The impossibility of what is virtual in our time and place is thus not a logical one like the proverbial round square, but a historical one—the impossibility of what is not yet or no longer possible for us to think, what is not yet or no longer possible for us "to inhabit."

It is thus "historical" in much the sense of Foucault's principle of singularity, that there are events in thought, and of that kind of genealogical critique that "will seek to treat the instances of discourse that articulate what we think, say, and do as so many historical events . . . that will not deduce from the form of what we know what is impossible for us to do and to know, but . . . will separate out, from the contingency that has made us what we are, the possibility of no longer being, doing, or thinking what we are, do, or think . . . the undefined work of freedom."[27]

That is why, commenting on Foucault's phrase "a history of the present," Deleuze calls him a philosopher of the "actual." *Actuel* can mean "of the present moment, existing, current"; *les actualités* are the news or current events. But the actuality of the "present" of which Foucault would write the history is something else, something "untimely."

For Foucault, writes Deleuze, "the actual is not what we are but rather what we become, what we are in the course of becoming, that is, the Other, our becoming-other. In every *dispositif*, it is necessary to distinguish what we are (what we are already no longer) from what we are in the course of becoming: the part of history, and the part of actuality."[28]

In analyzing the historical "singularity" of what we have been constructed to be (as subjects of discipline or of a normalized sexuality) Foucault would be "diagnosing" this present in which we are becoming something else. He would be tracing the lines of actualization of what we are not yet.

> The analysis of the archive . . . is valid for our diagnosis. Not because it would enable us to draw up a table of our distinctive features, and to sketch out in advance the face that we will have in the future. But it deprives us of our continuities; it dissipates that temporal identity in which we are pleased to look at ourselves when we wish to exercise the discontinuities of history.[29]

Foucault would be asking how to "inhabit" those moments of "actuality" in which we are becoming something else than what our history has constructed us to be, those heterotopic moments of our current historical "impossibility," the moments of invention.

In sum: we always become something other than who we are in the spaces we construct for ourselves to inhabit. It is the event of this *devenir-autre* that lets us see what is "uninhabitable" in those constructions, and so exposes them to our invention. And yet it does so without projecting a new order, or providing a new program of living. The necessity that compels us to interrupt our historical ways of habitation and to invent others is not a programmatic one. It is the point of disengagement from what we take for granted is required for us to be together in a proper time and place: *le point de folie*. It is from such points of folly that we may analyze the genealogy of the places assigned to our own self-constructions in those ways of inhabiting things we take as self-evident; and it is from them that we may start again the inventive task of constructing ourselves without arranging a mode of living, the task of our freedom. To diagnose what is happening to us is to trace, from the points of folly in our time and place, the lines of our actuality, of this Other we are becoming.

WHAT IS NEW IN ARCHITECTURE?

What is new in architecture; what is new in our building and our dwelling? That is a question that may be said to have obsessed our period of technological invention and possibility. It was a question central to the very concept of the avant-garde; for an avant-garde is by definition a group that carries forth a particular kind of novelty in our history.

And yet the avant-garde did not always conceive of what is new in the same manner.[30] Simplifying what is no doubt a much more complex history, one might say that the avant-garde did not conceive of novelty in terms of the "surprise" of "the event," and the space and time it involves. For the avant-garde wanted to itself be "the subject" of its novelty—master and possessor, and take upon itself to educate all others to the new order of habitation, of which it was the subject. What was new could thus be shown to all in pure visible form; it was not the novelty of this impure, disparate "multiplicity" of what cannot yet be seen, of this we who finds itself nowhere. For the avant-garde wished to resolve the tension between art and technological necessity by displaying "function" in visible "form," rather than trying to expose in given forms the tension with function that is the chance of an invention-to-come. The novelty that the avant-garde carried forth was, in short, a novelty not of historical invention, but of historical progression. It was, Derrida might say, a "novelty of the same"—the "new" of a "new order."[31] It invented "the possible from the possible," and was not (or could not know itself to be) an architecture of the "impossible."

The philosophical theme of "other time, other space" offers another way of thinking about what is new in architecture. An "architecture of the event" is an architecture not of the possible but of the actual, and so involves another idea of the new—the new is not the possible but the actual. The new is the "altogether-other" of our invention, the surprise of what is not yet possible in the histories of the spaces in which we find ourselves. It is not the invention of a possible form to be realized, but of this disparate virtuality of which we do not yet have the concept or which we cannot yet name. Of such novelty we are not the masters and possessors; we do not inhabit the "utopia" of what will be realized in history, but the "heterotopia" of those "lines of differentiation" that "actualize by inventing." That is why we can never find *ourselves* anywhere: our place is yet to come, our time is yet to take place. And the question of what is new in architecture thus becomes the question of how to inhabit this other time, this other place.

NOTES

1. "The Eye of Power," in *Power/Knowledge*, Colin Gordon, ed. (New York: Pantheon, 1980), pp. 149–50.

2. "Space, Knowledge, Power," in *Foucault Reader*, Rabinow, ed. (New York: Pantheon, 1984), p. 246.

3. "Preface to the *History of Sexuality*, Volume II," in *Foucault Reader*, p. 335. For a brief discussion of "event" and "singularity" in Foucault, see Pierre Macherey, "Foucault: éthique et subjectivité," in *Autrement* (Nov. 1988), no. 102, pp. 92–103.

4. Hacking, "Styles of Scientific Reasoning" in *Post-Analytic Philosophy*, Rajchman and West, eds., p. 155: ". . . styles of reasoning create the possibility for truth and falsehood. Deduction and induction merely preserve it." New York: Columbia University Press, 1985.

5. Foucault, *The Archeology of Knowledge* (New York: Harper, 1972), p. 28.

6. Foucault, "Of Other Spaces" *Diacritics* (Spring 1986), vol. 16, no. 1.

7. "Débat avec Michel Foucault," in *L'Impossible Prison* (Paris: Seuil, 1980), pp. 43–46.

8. Derrida, *Psyché: Invention de l'autre*, (Paris: Seuil, 1987) p. 15.

9. *Ibid.*, p. 9.

10. *Ibid.*, p. 35.

11. *Ibid.*, p. 10.

12. *Ibid.*, p. 37.

13. "The time of a Thesis; Punctuations" in *Philosophy in France Today*, Montefiori, ed. (Cambridge: Cambridge University Press, 1983), p. 44. It is interesting to note that the first of his own writings that Derrida dates is "Les fins de l'homme" of "Le 12 mai 1968," and that it ends with the question *"Mais qui, nous?"*

14. See Foucault's remarks about the departure of the new history from the attempt to " 'memorize the *monuments* of the past, transform them into *documents*" (*The Archeology of Knowledge*, pp. 7ff).

15. *Heimatlichkeit* in Hegel is the topic of Dominique Janicaud's book, *Hegel et le destin de la Grèce* (Paris: Vrin, 1975). Janicaud starts with this statement by Hegel: "Greece—in this name the heart of the civilized man of Europe, and of we Germans in particular, feels at home *(heimatlich)."* The Greeks were the first to build for themselves a world that was their own; and this Greek *Heimatlichkeit* is the same one that leads we civilized Europeans, and especially we Germans to our Western *Heimat*. For Spirit is *not yet* at home in the Greek home; that requires the building and *Bildung* of History. Hegel's discussion of architecture is connected to this general scheme of Spirit returning to its *Heimat*. The reference to "we Germans in particular" would help to explain why Hegel's conception of classical architecture remains entirely Greek, with no mention of the Italian Renaissance. Derrida's early discussion of the Egyptian pyramid that would house the basically *unheimlich* body of the mummy is connected to this larger questioning of the scheme of History returning to its Home.

16. Derrida, *Psyché*, p. 514.

17. *Ibid.*, p. 60.

18. *Ibid.*, p. 478.

19. On the concept of freedom see Jean-Luc Nancy, *L'Expérience de la liberté* (Paris: Galilée, 1988). My *Michel Foucault: The Freedom of Philosophy* (New York: Columbia University Press, 1985) also takes the concept of freedom as a central one.

20. Derrida, *Psyché*, p. 489.

21. *Ibid.*, p. 55.

22. *Ibid.*, pp. 535–596.

23. Deleuze, *Bergsonism* (New York: Zone, 1988), p. 97.

24. Nelson Goodman's famous second paradox of induction is designed to show that there can be no induction without "entrenchment" of the predicates that describe the world in which one explains or predicts. It follows that events can be said to be more or less probable only for a "version of the world," which cannot itself be said, or be said in the same manner, to be more or less probable. The Deleuzian idea of event is thus something like the event of a new version of the world in our thinking; and his idea of "multiplicity" is like the notion of the disunity of such versions. In another context Ian Hacking remarks: "Leibniz said that God chose a world which maximized the variety of phenomena while choosing the simplest laws. Exactly so: but the best way to maximize phenomena and

have simplest laws is to have the laws inconsistent with each other, each applying to this or that but none applying to all." *Representing and Intervening* (Cambridge: Cambridge University Press, 1983), p. 219.

25. Deleuze, *Bergsonism*, p. 101.

26. *Ibid.*, p. 103.

27. "What Is Enlightenment," in *Foucault Reader*, p. 14.

28. Deleuze, "Foucault, historien du présent," in *Michel Foucault, philosophe* (Paris: Seuil, 1989). (I discuss this Deleuzian formulation in "Crisis," *Representations* (Fall 1989), no. 28.

29. Foucault, *The Archeology of Knowledge*, pp. 130–31.

30. De Duve argues that Duchamp was not a utopian: the "time" of the invention of the ready-made was not that of a new plastic order, but of an "abandonment" of such an order. (See preceding essay.)

31. In *Psyché*, p. 475, Derrida remarks in passing that the now frequent use of "post" in "postmodernism" or "poststructuralism" still remains hostage to a "historicist compulsion," a "progressivist ideology." Thus the postmodern would break with the modern only in terms of the progressivist conception of a break characteristic of the modern; as such it would not have the time or the novelty of an event.

INDEX

Index